PENGUIN BOO

A Friend for Life

Battersea Dogs & Cats Home would like to thank all of the contributors to this book for sharing their stories and photographs.

A Friend for Life

BATTERSEA DOGS
& CATS HOME
with PUNTEHA VAN
TERHEYDEN

PENGUIN BOOKS

PENGUIN BOOKS

UK | USA | Canada | Ireland | Australia
India | New Zealand | South Africa

Penguin Books is part of the Penguin Random House group of companies
whose addresses can be found at global.penguinrandomhouse.com

Penguin
Random House
UK

First published 2016

001

Copyright © Battersea Dogs & Cats Home, 2016

The moral right of the author has been asserted

Produced under licence from Battersea Dogs Home Ltd® Battersea Dogs & Cats Home

Royalties from the sale of this book go towards supporting the work of Battersea Dogs & Cats Home

Battersea Dogs & Cats Home has been caring for and rehoming abandoned, stray and neglected
animals since 1860. We have looked after over 3 million dogs and cats since then, and we aim never to
turn away an animal in need of our help. To find out more about our charity visit battersea.org.uk

Set in 12.75/15pt Garamond MT Std

Typeset in India by Thomson Digital Pvt Ltd, Noida, Delhi

Printed in Great Britain by Clays Ltd, St Ives plc

A CIP catalogue record for this book is available from the British Library

ISBN: 978-1-405-92559-4

www.greenpenguin.co.uk

Contents

Foreword by Paul O'Grady

Every year thousands of unwanted, abandoned and lost animals find themselves at one of Battersea Dogs & Cats Home's three rehoming centres. Some arrive with heart-breaking stories of cruelty and neglect whereas others simply cannot be looked after any more by their owners and are brought to Battersea as a last option. There are also many bewildered dogs and cats that arrive as strays with backgrounds that can only be guessed at.

Arriving at Battersea may seem like a sad ending but, more often than not, it is the best possible outcome for these animals and represents the start of a journey to find a new owner, a new home and a new life. No matter how long that journey may take, Battersea's dedicated staff and army of volunteers will be on hand to provide the very best of care at every step of the way. Of course, it isn't just as simple as finding every Battersea resident a new place to live: each animal is carefully matched to the new owner's situation and lifestyle to make sure they are a good fit.

For every dog or cat saved from an unhappy situation, or from an uncertain future, there is, of course, a human story too. I have personally talked with many people who have adopted a Battersea animal and they tell me how their new arrivals quickly settle into their new surroundings and become one of the family, changing the household for the better. It goes to show how a family pet can really make a house a home and bring comfort, happiness and love to a person's life.

Sometimes the impact of rehoming a dog or cat goes beyond companionship, and the animals that are adopted from Battersea Dogs & Cats Home may in turn emotionally rescue their new owners from loneliness or even depression. The stories in this book show how rewarding pet ownership can be.

I firmly believe that sharing your house with an animal is good for both pet and owner and I certainly can't imagine not having my five dogs around. My home would feel totally empty without them, and they bring me as much comfort and happiness as I hope they get from sharing my home with me. They can certainly lift my mood when I need it – take it from me that a furry face or two welcoming you on the doorstep can do wonders for your well-being!

As a nation of animal lovers, we are lucky to have such amazing animal rescue centres dedicated to giving our four-legged friends a second chance. Battersea Dogs & Cats Home remains a much-loved and, sadly, much-needed national treasure, which relies on the generosity of the public to help it to continue to look after the animals in its care.

If you would like to support the work that Battersea does or are interested in rehoming a dog or cat, please visit www.battersea.org.uk.

Paul

Amazing Grace

I sat down on the sofa and stared across the room at my husband, John, willing him to change his mind. We'd been debating something important for months now and I could tell we were on the home stretch. 'Come on, John, let's get Ali a kitten. She's eleven now and I know she'll do a great job taking care of it.'

Our two daughters, Shelley, fourteen, and Alison, had never wanted for anything apart from a pet cat and now, as Christmas loomed ever closer, I hoped John would agree to grant Ali her wish.

'But what about when we go on holiday, Irene? It's not fair to leave the cat somewhere else for days on end.'

I told him we'd ask a neighbour to cat-sit, or we'd find the best cattery in town. 'Please, John,' I said. 'Ali's been pining for a pet to call her own for years now. I think she's ready.'

'Well, it would be good for her to have that responsibility,' he conceded.

A smile began to form on his face but it didn't begin at his lips. As the corners of his sparkly blue eyes crinkled, I knew I had him.

'Oh, all right, then,' he said. 'It probably is about time.'

We set about planning. Ali loved watching *Bagpuss* on the television and dreamt of having a big tomcat. I searched and searched but nothing was quite right. Weeks later, I heard from friends of a three-month-old short-haired silver kitten in desperate need of a loving home.

Soon I was able to pick her up and drove straight to my sister-in-law Jeannie's house. We'd decided to call her Holly because it was nearly Christmas. Holly was shaking like a leaf and to comfort her I placed her next to Toby, Jeannie's tiny King Charles Cavalier puppy. They curled up on the sofa against each other and fell asleep.

I knew Holly was in safe hands for the next week at Jeannie's house, so I prepared our home for her arrival. I bought a cat bed, collar and food, and stashed them in the garage. Only John would brave the biting December cold to potter around in there – it was his favourite part of our home – and it was the only place Ali would fail to search for any Christmas presents.

On Christmas morning, we had breakfast as usual, then got ready for our family to arrive. I'd already briefed Shelley on the plan and she was very excited, and really looking forward to seeing her little sister's face when our new arrival made her entrance.

When the doorbell rang at eleven o'clock, I said, 'Ali, go and answer that, please. It'll be Auntie Jeannie.'

Ali raced into the hall while John, Shelley and I gathered behind her. As she pulled open the front door, Jeannie stood on the step with her arms folded across her chest.

'This is a present for you,' she said.

'Oh!' Ali squealed. 'Look, Mum, it's my own Bagpuss!' She stepped aside to let us see. There, tucked into Jeannie's arms, was little Holly, her eyes peeping out at us.

'I wish you could see your faces right now,' Jeannie said. 'You're all grinning like the Cheshire Cat.'

Our guests came inside, but Ali was too scared to take tiny Holly into her arms. We moved to the living room where Jeannie placed her gently on the floor. As soon as her paws hit the carpet she scooted behind the sofa and hid. 'She's frightened,' Ali observed.

With some coaxing, patience and tasty treats, we finally got her out.

The rest of the Christmas presents didn't get a look in that year as our girls fussed over the newest addition to our family. It was a very special time.

Despite John's earlier anxiety about getting a pet for Ali, he knew, as I did, that we'd made the right call. I'd known in my heart it would all work fine because I knew my husband inside out. John and I had met at the local dance hall when I was sixteen. We married when I was twenty, and he was twenty-seven. When the girls came along, our family had finally seemed complete. It wasn't until now that I realized a little someone had been missing – Holly.

Years passed and Holly was very much Ali's cat. We'd told her from the beginning that Holly was her responsibility and she hadn't let us down. Ali fed her, groomed her and gave her all the love in the world. She even saved up dozens of cat-food coupons to get a special gift: a blue velvet cushion for Holly to sleep on in her bedroom. In return, Holly was her right-hand cat.

I'd be in the kitchen cooking and I'd step out to call everyone to dinner, only to hear music blasting from all over the house. John would be in the lounge listening to his favourite jazz and the girls would be upstairs in their respective bedrooms, playing their own records. They all drove me mad, as well as each other, with their varied tastes, but the only person who had an ally in all the craziness was Ali. Holly followed her wherever she went. The two would cuddle up in her room and listen to music or watch TV together.

We all had a soft spot for Holly. John would scoop her into his arms and talk to her in whispers. He'd stroll to the window and, stroking her under the chin, would gaze outside. 'Look at that horrible rain, girl. Aren't you glad you're here with me instead?'

Holly would purr her agreement.

Our Holly-cat spent many wonderful years being spoilt by everyone in the house, and when the girls moved to a flat in London, Ali returned every week-end to visit. I liked to tell myself that she'd come to see me and John, but she'd race into the house and call for Holly. Her cat would come running to her as if she hadn't seen her for a year. It was clear the two pined for each other during the week but the girls' landlord wouldn't let them have any pets so John and I took care of Holly.

One weekend over breakfast, we noticed Holly was struggling to get her back legs up and out of the cat flap.

'She's getting old,' John said.

By then Holly was eighteen and had lived longer than any of us could have imagined. None of us wanted to think of the difficult decision that would be upon us soon enough, but Ali always insisted, 'It has to be me. I'll take her to the vet when it is time.'

Later that morning, John disappeared into the garage. The hours ticked by and I took him a cup of tea. He was banging and sawing and sanding, with chunks of wood and dust flying everywhere.

'Are you ever coming in?' I said.

He grinned. 'I'm making a step for the cat.'

John had always been a wonderful dad and husband, fixing everything around the house, helping the neighbours and decorating the girls' rooms no matter how often they wanted a change. It was really no surprise that now they were living away he had turned his attention to Holly.

I couldn't help but wind him up a bit. 'You didn't even want a cat all those years ago,' I said.

'I know,' he smiled. 'But I do love the old girl.'

A short while later, Ali and I gathered in the kitchen to watch John install the pyramid cat-ramp he had fashioned. It meant Holly could step up to the cat flap, push through it and step down the other side with ease. It was perfect.

A year later, even the ramp couldn't help Holly. She lost the power in her back legs and one day became distressed. We made the call we'd been dreading. The vet agreed to come to the house and we all waited anxiously in the lounge.

Eventually I heard a car pull into the driveway and my heart sank. The doorbell rang and Ali stood up. 'I'll get it.'

It was nearly twenty years since that doorbell had rung on Christmas Day and Ali had answered it to say hello to her kitten. Now she showed the vet in and took Holly into her arms. 'I have to hold Holly as she goes,' she said.

The vet set to work, gently explaining each step to Ali as he went. I couldn't bear it and neither could John. He shut himself into the bathroom and I went into the kitchen. Afterwards we all hugged each other and cried, and I vowed I'd never have another cat. It was too painful.

Ali returned to London and, in time, Shelley moved to Chicago for work. It was supposed to be for eighteen months but she stayed longer as her career in advertising soared. John and I were proud of both our girls and missed having them in the house, but we found new things to keep us busy. Ali got a cat and began fostering moggies in need. John and I retired, went on lovely holidays and pottered in the garden. We spent time with friends and neighbours and nipped down to the local pub whenever we could.

One summer we helped Ali buy a place in London and spent the last week of August that year moving her in. John built her a loft ladder and fitted it. He was seventy-two but still fit as a fiddle.

Then, one morning, he went downstairs as I was making the bed. 'Coffee?' he called up to me.

'Yes, please!' I shouted back.

Seconds later I heard a massive crash and rushed downstairs, my heart hammering. I found John lying flat on his back, eyes wide open. He didn't appear to be breathing so I dialled 999. Soon an ambulance arrived. The paramedics worked to revive him and he began to stir. That was when we realized that he had hit his head on the worktop as he collapsed and his head was bleeding. He was rushed to hospital, very confused and speaking gibberish.

A scan revealed bad news.

I called Ali. 'Dad's not well. The doctors think there's a tumour in his brain.'

She took a cab all the way home to Maidenhead, and Shelley took the first flight home from Chicago.

Meanwhile John was transferred to the John Radcliffe Hospital in Oxfordshire for brain surgery.

7

Ten hours later, we learnt that he'd had a massive bleed in his brain but there was no tumour. We were told to expect the worst. Somehow, though, he managed to pull through. The next few months were spent first in hospital, then rehabilitation centres. Ali had to return to London and Shelley went back to Chicago.

During that time, without my family and without Holly, the house felt very lonely. Sometimes when I visited John, I'd stare at a beautiful painting of a sunset on the wall in his hospital room and wish we were somewhere else looking at that instead of where we were.

It was a long and difficult journey and John was confused at times. Sometimes, he'd wander off in his pyjamas late at night, unaware of why he was being kept in hospital, and the police would find him sitting in the pub with a half-pint of Guinness, wondering why everyone was staring at him.

It was difficult to see him in that confused state, but I was sure that the resourceful man I'd fallen in love with all those years earlier was still in there somewhere. Finally, after nine hard months and weekly visits from us, I was able to bring John home. When he walked into our house, he was so relieved to be back that we hugged each other for the longest time. Later he'd tell our friends about his pyjama-clad escapades, making himself and everybody else laugh. My John was back, as was Shelley from Chicago, and the four of us took a little holiday to Wales.

Slowly, John was able to get back into his beloved garage. One evening, I noticed he'd developed a cough and thought he'd been out in the cold too long. Weeks passed and five times the doctor insisted it was a virus. But finally I said, 'John, you must get that cough checked out properly.'

He was referred for an X-ray. Two days later we were called into our local surgery for the result. In the consulting room, the doctor said reluctantly, 'I'm very sorry but you have lung cancer.'

We sat there in disbelief. 'But I don't smoke,' he said. 'I never have. Which lung is it?'

'Both.'

Shelley came home once more and the four of us went to see John's oncologist. He was matter-of-fact and went straight to the point: 'I suggest you have a nice holiday and get your affairs in order, John. You have months, not years.'

The cancer had already spread to his hip and spine, and it was too late for chemotherapy. It was a terrible blow after the horrible months John had had to spend in hospital recovering from brain surgery.

That night we climbed into bed and held hands till the sun rose. We talked through our tears and the next day we had a plan.

We booked a two-week holiday on an island in the Canaries and the four of us, with our neighbours Tony and Jean, jetted off together for a much-needed break. When we arrived at the resort, we were shown to a penthouse suite with a huge kitchen, dining room and lounge. It had a wraparound balcony with a jacuzzi and three bedrooms. We drank champagne in the hot tub and spent hours talking about anything but the cancer. At times it was hard to believe that John was so ill.

When we got home, we spent a special Christmas together and the doctor arranged for a hospital bed to be delivered to our home. We took care of John there, and all of his friends came to visit. Jazz music played, and John told stories, everybody laughing. On 30 January 2013, the girls and I gathered around John's bed and held his hands as he smiled at us, then slipped peacefully away.

Somehow, we ploughed ahead and arranged his funeral. The girls penned beautiful tributes and the church was packed: more than three hundred people came to pay their respects as Frank Sinatra songs and John's favourite Welsh hymns played. The service marked the end of his life, and the end of forty-seven happy years of marriage.

Afterwards, my friends dropped in and kept in touch by phone, but no matter how many people I spoke to, I felt increasingly alone. My girls were amazing but I understood they had their own lives to lead. Sometimes I'd wake at four a.m. and the silence of my home was deafening. John was gone and loneliness was my new reality. I felt isolated and developed a bizarre anger that I couldn't hold in. I tried counselling and bereavement groups but nothing seemed to help.

By now, Ali had two cats. 'Come on, Mum,' she'd say. 'Why won't you get a cat? You'll feel so much happier.'

'I don't want one. I'm not ready.'

She didn't give up. Every call we shared consisted of Ali going on about me getting a cat for company, and me angrily batting her off.

As the one-year anniversary of John's death loomed, Ali came over with her iPad and pulled up the website of Battersea Dogs & Cats Home. She clicked on the cats page and began looking through the profiles. She stopped when she saw a ginger cat.

'Ali, I don't want a cat.' I sighed.

'Please, Mum, let's just go and have a look together.'

I got into a huff and stomped upstairs. Eventually Ali went to bed. Unable to sleep, I picked up my own iPad and browsed through Battersea's pages. As I looked at all the cat profiles, I thought, *Maybe this isn't a bad idea after all*, though I didn't admit it to Ali until later.

In time, Ali drove me to Battersea's site in Old Windsor and we walked through the cattery, reading the profiles and peering into the pens. It was a week-end, and most of the cats had been snapped up. Then I saw a cat called Russell in his pen. The lovely young lady who had been showing us around asked if I'd like to meet him.

I nodded but just as we were about to step inside, Russell slipped from his tray and splashed into his water, sending it flying everywhere. As our guide set about clearing it up, I glanced into the pen next to his. It looked empty but the label on the window said: *Grace*.

'What about this little one?' I asked.

She laughed. 'She's not so little! Would you like to meet her?'

Again, I nodded. I went in, sat down and Grace began to emerge from her hiding place. Her long black body seemed to go on for ever. She was a Norwegian Forest Cat and absolutely gorgeous, with piercing yellow eyes as big as saucers. I reached out my hand for her to sniff, slowly, so as not to startle her, and Grace put her wet nose against my fingers. We stayed like that for a moment, neither moving, then Grace pushed forcefully on my hand and rubbed her cheek against it.

Ali and I glanced at each other. 'She's timid but she isn't hiding,' I said.

Ali grinned. 'Mum, she's your cat. I really like her.'

By now, Grace was purring around my legs.

There was such a sense of peacefulness with Grace, that, for the first time in months, I stopped thinking about John and how ill he had been, how much I missed him and how I had nobody to go home to. The anger that had been bubbling inside me since he'd died seemed to ebb away, leaving only a serenity I hadn't felt for a long time.

I was smitten with Grace, and Ali stepped outside to give us a few minutes together. It was as though the world around us disappeared. Grace gave me so much love and warmth that I wanted to pull her onto my lap but I didn't dare push my luck. After all, we'd only just met.

There was a cautious neediness about Grace, a bit like me, I suppose. I knew in my heart that she was meant to be my cat because when I was with her the horrible ache inside me went away.

Ali stepped back inside and whispered, 'How do you feel now, Mum? Are you still angry with me?'

I shook my head. 'Not at all. I really love her.'

Suddenly she seemed a bit flustered. 'We can go home and have a think about it, Mum. I feel like I've pushed you into it.'

I tried to reassure her: 'You did push me initially but this is my decision. I really want this cat. I have to have her.'

We left Grace in her pen and returned to talk to the Battersea lady, whose name was Leah. I was asked several questions and talked a lot about Holly – even mentioning the ramp John had made for her. 'The cat flap is still there,' I added. Then a question occurred to me. 'What is Grace's background?'

Leah told us that Grace had been badly bullied by her sister, who had been very dominant. She had forced Grace, now three years and eight months old, out of the house more and more and her owners had realized that Grace was scared of her sister and never had any peace. 'Grace's sister made it plain that she didn't want Grace around and was being very nasty. Grace isn't forceful enough to deal with that. Her owners were very upset but knew it was best to find her a loving home.'

I learnt that Grace's previous owners had left her with a beautiful wicker basket and a scratching post, and hoped for an update once she was settled with a new family. I was more than happy to provide that, so I gave permission for my contact details to be sent to them.

Grace had just had work done on her teeth at the Battersea clinic and was up to date with all her shots, so she was fine to come home with me. Normally, the process takes a bit longer but Battersea were satisfied that Grace and I were a suitable match. We would keep in touch by telephone as Battersea needed to check that everything was going well.

On the way home, I drove the car while Ali held Grace's basket. She talked to her all the way to keep her calm. When we arrived, we set Grace down in the living room and she came out cautiously. After a few moments, she scooted behind the sofa, like Holly had all those years earlier, but it wasn't long before she came out, jumped on the sofa, lay down on Ali's lap and promptly fell asleep. I was amazed but it also made sense: I felt as if Grace had been mine all her life. It was clear that she felt the same about us.

For the first two nights Grace slept upstairs on John's side of the bed. When I woke in the middle of the night from a bad dream, Grace's big paw was on my hand. It was as if she had been holding it while I slept. I wanted to grab my mobile phone and take a picture to show Ali but Grace woke up and rolled over. The moment passed in the blink of an eye but the feeling of comfort lingered.

Two weeks later, Ali came to see us and remarked on how chirpy I was. 'I told you a cat was what you needed. Look at the difference Grace has made to you!'

The stubborn part of my personality, which I had passed on to Ali, made me want to deny that my new happiness was down to Grace but I couldn't. I no longer found myself putting off coming home or even getting out of bed in the morning because I knew Grace would be waiting for me with love and cuddles.

The house felt alive again with Grace's miaows, her purring and the soft sound of her paws as she ran around for a crazy minute, or if she heard Ali's voice call for her through the phone. Even her toys brightened the place up. It was nice to walk into a room and find it different from how I had left it. It made me feel less alone. Grace had a favourite white toy mouse that had come with her from Battersea and she carried it around everywhere. I found it in the kitchen, on the stairs, on the sofa. I sent pictures of Grace sprawled on the carpet and an email about her progress to the Home:

> Grace has settled in perfectly and we are both really happy to be getting to know each other. Please let Grace's previous family know that I promise to look after her. She's already made such a difference in my life and I can assure you she will be ruined with affection. I love her to pieces.

Before long, I had a forwarded response from Grace's previous owners:

> Dear Irene, thank you for your lovely message. We were so upset when we had to give Grace up but it looks like she has found the peace and comfort she truly deserves with you.

We sent messages and pictures back and forth, talking about Grace and what a special girl she was. It felt so nice to make new friends. It was almost as though John had sent Grace to me, opening up my world again to new experiences and new people.

I later recalled that the day we visited Battersea, we had bumped into a mother and daughter on our way out: they had come to see Grace after spotting her profile online. If I hadn't finally given in to Ali, I might have missed Grace that day. The thought sends a shiver down my spine.

Grace and I spend hours together. We sit on the sofa while I watch my soaps, and she pushes right up against me. We go into the garden together and chase each other around. We play football and, although I'm seventy, I can still give Grace a run for her money when it comes to hide and seek. She has brought so much sunshine and laughter into my life and we have lots of fun together. There are even times when Grace is my counsellor. I talk to her about John, and if I'm feeling sad, she senses it and makes sure to hang around me for extra cuddles.

Not too long ago I woke in the middle of the night, screaming, from a nightmare. As I sat on the edge of the bed trying to shake away the awful dream, Grace appeared in the doorway to check on me. Then she jumped up on the bed and stared at me until I was ready to lie down. As soon as my head hit the pillow, she curled up against my stomach and stayed there for the rest of the night. She has so much heart and such a caring nature.

Since Grace came to live with me, she has changed my life immeasurably. Before Grace, I was depressed and lonely. Now I feel lighter and happier. I found it hard to be at home after losing John. Now I can't get back quick enough when I've been out. I was annoyed with Ali when she was pushing me towards taking in a cat but my advice to anyone reading this who has lost the person they love is: just think of what a pet could bring you. The joy you feel when you have an animal to care for is immense. They have their own personalities and, like us humans, are unique.

When I am with friends and they ask if I'd like to stay overnight instead of going home, I say, 'No, thank you. I want to get home and see Grace.'

My home is no longer silent, and that's down to my amazing Grace.

Frank Says Relax

I looked around at all the boxes, packed with our belongings, and felt a pang of guilt. My husband, Scott, had been urging me to move into our new home for nearly four months but something was stopping me making the move from my parents' house to our new flat up the road. That something was actually a someone: my dog, Remi.

My English Bull Terrier was fourteen years old and I'd had her from when she was a puppy. Before my brother Daniel had gone to university, he'd had a dog too, Baggy, who was Remi's sister. As Daniel and I had grown up, our dogs had grown with us. We had journeyed through our lives together and now Dad was taking care of Baggy. I could have taken Remi with me and moved in with Scott but it wouldn't have been fair on the dogs. The sisters were too old to be split up now.

The thought of leaving Remi behind with my parents at their home in Essex made my heart ache. So, instead of dealing with the separation, I put off moving, giving Scott one excuse after another: 'We need to get those windows replaced first . . . Let's redecorate the flat, get it all perfect, then move in.'

Every time, he let out a sigh and smiled knowingly. We both knew the reason I wasn't ready to make the move and he was gentle with me.

I worked at a school nearby, so every lunchtime I popped home to see Remi and take her for a walk. In the evenings, my dad, Brian, did the honours. He loved her and Baggy as much as my brother and I did. Throughout my adolescence, I'd taken Remi to my friends' homes or to play in the park. As I'd got older, she'd come in the car with me wherever I went and was next to me when I caught up with friends at the pub. She had been a huge part of my life and the thought of living in a flat without a dog was too much to take.

Then, one sunny Sunday morning, I had an idea. 'Do you fancy a look around Battersea Dogs & Cats Home?' I asked Scott.

He looked up the opening hours. 'It opens at ten. Let's go after breakfast.'

An hour later we were at the gates. I wasn't really sure what kind of dog I was looking for until I saw Frank, a brindled Staffordshire Bull Terrier. He was bouncing up and down with excitement. We stopped to stay hello. 'He looks cheeky, doesn't he?' I said to Scott.

He agreed. 'What about this beautiful Husky, though?' He pointed to a gorgeous white Inuit standing proudly in the kennel next door. He was much calmer than Frank and really quite majestic. They were both beautiful dogs, but when I glanced back at Frank, something about his face made me smile. I had always been a fan of bull breeds and I could tell Frank had a lovely personality.

Scott and I continued our tour, and after a while we decided to go for an assessment to find out if Battersea thought we'd make suitable owners. We figured there was no harm in trying. We registered our details, and Ellie, who worked there, interviewed us to learn about our experience with dogs, our working hours, our home situation and our property. Then she said, 'Did you like any of the dogs you saw today?'

'Yes,' I said. 'We liked the look of two.'

She didn't ask which ones. Instead she explained that they liked to try to match the dog to us, rather than give us the dog we wanted: each dog is rehomed to a family who can cater for all its needs. Ellie tapped on her computer and after a while she said: 'I think I have the perfect dog for you. His name is Frank.'

'The Staffie?' I said.

'That's the one,' came the reply. It felt like fate.

We were taken to a room to meet Frank, and moments later the door opened. A familiar black-and-ginger shape bounded in. Ellie unclipped Frank's lead and he rushed straight past me to the far corner of the room where a box of toys sat waiting. He snuffled around the box, then took as many as he could in his mouth. He trotted back to me, dumped the items at my feet and sat down promptly. He stared at me then, as if to say, *Come on, aren't you going to play with me?*

In that moment, I knew Frank was coming home with us. Scott felt the same and we told Ellie we'd take him, if we were allowed to. She started filling out the paperwork and told us somebody would visit our home during the next week. We agreed, of course, then learnt some more about Frank's background.

He was six months old but, sadly, his previous owners hadn't been able to devote the hours needed to help Frank with his separation anxiety, an emotional and behavioural problem dogs can suffer from if left alone for too long. They are naturally sociable animals and the thousands of years they have spent working and living with humans has made some dogs sensitive to being alone. I was determined to put in the time and effort Frank needed from me.

I explained that the school where I worked was just up the road from our new home and I would be out for a maximum of two hours at a time. I'd pop home for lunch and a walk at midday, go back to school for one o'clock, then be home again by three. I knew I could make it work. I wasn't going to let him go to another family because, quite simply, he had stolen my heart.

Six hours after we'd arrived at Battersea, we were able to take Frank home with us. It was unusual but, as we lived quite far away, it was deemed the best option. We were reminded that a member of the Battersea rehoming team would visit our house to check it was suitable for Frank.

We set off and drove straight home to Mum and Dad's to introduce our new arrival. Frank, Remi and Baggy sniffed each other but didn't show much more interest so Scott and I decided to walk over to the park. Just before we left the house, I stopped Scott and told him to grab the keys to our new flat. His eyebrows shot up but he said no more.

We kept Frank on the lead as we didn't know how good his recall was and didn't want to risk him running away or having to chase him all over the place. He was very excited and pulled on the lead quite a bit, but I knew I'd have that under control soon enough.

When Frank was as worn out as we were, we walked over to our ground-floor maisonette. Most of our belongings were there already, and for the first time since we'd bought it, we spent the night in our home. As we settled down to sleep, Scott said, 'If I had known it would take a dog to get you here, Rachel, I would have found you one months ago!'

It was hard being away from Remi but having Frank to greet me in the morning made it easier. Time passed and we all settled in, but Frank did find it hard to be alone. Even though it was never more than a couple of hours, I'd come home to find the loo roll shredded, poo behind the front door and the door trims pulled off. But I knew I had to persevere. If I didn't put in the time to teach Frank that I would always come home to him, his anxiety would never ease.

Whenever I was at school, I left the radio playing for Frank and made sure the bathroom door was shut. When I got home, I'd play with him for hours, take him to see my parents and get him used to socializing. I bought lots of toys to occupy him and keep his mind off me when I was out. I hoped all the extra love and care would do the trick. But eighteen months after we'd brought him home, Frank was still struggling. Whenever he became fearful, he was destructive. I knew that I would never give up on him, so I did some reading and spoke to friends who had dogs. One suggested I get Frank a crate. In the past, I hadn't been keen on the idea but now I figured anything was worth a try.

I placed the crate in the hallway, with his bed inside. Frank was watching me curiously and as soon as I stepped aside he rushed in and sank into his bed. From that moment on, he calmed down completely. I realized he hadn't felt safe until I'd got the crate and that was why he became so fretful when I was out. The crate gave him a safe haven and a sense of security. It was a breakthrough for us and I was chuffed to bits to see the positive change in him. In the evenings Frank slept in his crate, always with the door open.

Around the same time, I signed Frank up to obedience classes. He loved doing them so much that I signed up for an agility course too. He thoroughly enjoyed the stimulation and it helped us bond even more. Also, he was really good at it. He was a natural at obedience because he was such a smart boy. Sometimes, when it came to the agility, the movement and running around got him a bit overexcited and he'd dart off to run laps around the course to burn off some of his energy. I wondered if I should stop the agility and focus on the obedience, but then I remembered how my continued effort to understand Frank had led us to the crate. I wanted to put in a lot of effort with him so I persisted with both.

That wasn't to say Frank didn't drive me mad sometimes.

He'd run in circles and bark with excitement. 'Oh, Frank!' I'd say. 'Will you come here!' Eventually he'd come to heel and look very pleased with himself.

The hours I put in paid off. Two years on, Frank won a prize at the training school's annual awards ceremony. He puffed out his chest and I beamed with pride as he was given treats and we accepted the accolade of Best Agility Dog and Best Handler.

Frank joined the Battersea Agility Display Team after I went to a reunion at Old Windsor and he won a Best Trick class. One of the handlers saw Frank's potential and put me in touch with Ali, who dealt with the team. Frank was a shoo-in for a place on it and flourished. He loved taking part in the displays: going over jumps, through tunnels and weaves, over dog walks and A-frames. His skills were endless. Being on the team led to other opportunities too, like magazine shoots and appearances on *Paul O'Grady: For the Love of Dogs*. Frank went around the agility course at a dog show with Paul himself. I was so very proud.

While my relationship and bond with Frank went from strength to strength, somebody else was becoming weaker in body and mind. My darling Remi was an old girl now and was no longer interested in going for walks with me and Frank. Instead, she liked to sleep a lot and relax in her twilight years. Eventually, she passed away, as did Baggy.

She left a hole in my life that I couldn't quite bear. It was lucky that, just recently, I had taken in Roxy, an English Bull Terrier, from Bull Breed Rescue. It was good for Frank to have a new friend. But Roxy was a scabby mess who had been terribly mistreated. She had demodectic mange and her coat had fallen out, but her personality shone through.

She and Frank became the best of friends and happily trotted alongside one another on walks. They liked to nap together too. Whenever we went out in the car the two of them sat happily in the back until we reached our destination.

I only ever had trouble with Roxy when it was bath time. And who could blame her? She needed daily medicated baths and quickly caught on that a visit to the bathroom meant the smelly shampoo would come out. She started to run and hide in her crate when six p.m. loomed. She'd squash herself into a corner so that I couldn't get her out, which was very distressing for everyone. I hated doing it to her, Roxy hated me doing it to her, and Frank fretted that we were both upset, pacing around us as, every evening, the drama unfolded. In time, however, Roxy's skin healed and those horrible chemical baths became a thing of the past.

Frank and Roxy played tug-of-war and on walks they ran across the fields together like the wind. Yet, whenever they needed to be well behaved and calm, they were as good as gold.

One Christmas, when a teacher at school asked if I'd bring my dogs in to meet the children, I didn't hesitate to say yes. The children had special needs and some suffered with painful physical problems. I hoped seeing the dogs would be fun for them and provide a brief escape from their difficulties.

On the designated morning, I pulled open my chest of fancy-dress items and Roxy and Frank appeared beside me with their tails wagging. They both knew that a fun day lay ahead. I dressed them in matching reindeer outfits and we set off for school. They were excited and a bit hyper as we walked to work because

26

they knew those outfits meant they were about to receive lots of fuss and cuddles. But as soon as we went through the doors into the school, they fell into step beside me and were as cool as cucumbers.

The dogs sat next to Father Christmas, who had come to see the children for a festive assembly. Afterwards, the children came forward in small groups to meet Frank and Roxy. I noticed a boy in a wheelchair staring at them. He had cerebral palsy and limited mobility so I took the dogs over to him. 'Would you like to stroke Frank?' I asked. He gave a slight nod so I gently placed his hand on Frank's back. Frank didn't move an inch. It was as if he knew the child next to him had trouble with his hands: his fingers were clenched tightly and the tendons stuck out with the strain of the spasms in his muscles. I felt terribly sad for him, but as he sat with his hand on Frank, I noticed something amazing. The tension in it began to ease as the muscles relaxed. Fifteen minutes later, the boy was able to put his now open hand flat on Frank's back and stroke him. His beaming smile said it all.

As the years went by, Roxy and Frank became a firm fixture at my school. The staff and children all loved them. The feeling was mutual and Frank in particular adored children. Whenever one came to visit or he saw one in the park, he'd quite happily ditch me for them! Once, we were walking by a lake when Frank ran off. I called and called him to no avail. Then I spotted him across the lake, playing with a family. I made my way over and found him on his back, having his belly rubbed. I apologized to the family and we all had a good laugh. Frank was very pleased with himself – that much was clear to all of us.

Not all families were like that one by the lake. Some parents would see Roxy and Frank and pull their children away, or cross the road to avoid us. It wasn't their fault that they didn't know enough about bull breeds to recognize that mine were under control and very well trained. But there were other times, too, when Frank and Roxy would face unfair prejudice and I wanted every single person who judged my dogs on the way they looked to understand the joy of having them as well-trained pets.

Ironically, it happened a lot when I took them to dog shows to compete in agility or obedience competitions. I often heard parents say to their children, of Frank and Roxy, 'Watch out. That dog will bite you. Keep away from it.' Sometimes I'd let it go, but at others I found myself telling them, 'That's not the thing to say because you'll scare your children for no good reason.'

Hours later, when my dogs appeared dressed up as a bride and groom, or in whatever costume I'd taken for them, the same parents would be straight over, asking if their children could pose with Roxy and Frank for a picture or two.

That came to mind when one of the instructors at our obedience training class approached me one evening – even though my two didn't need any more training, they enjoyed going so much that I went every week for many years. She asked if I'd be interested in involving Roxy in a cynophobia class. Cynophobia is the fear of dogs and she ran a class on Wednesday evenings for children. 'I think Roxy would be perfect for it. The children who come to my classes need to see all sorts of dogs if they're really going to get over their fear and Roxy is an unusual-looking dog. You don't see many English Bull Terriers around and, for a child with a phobia, she can look a bit scary.'

I understood where she was coming from. 'She's such a softie, though.'

'I know. That's why she's perfect for this course. Will you give it some thought?'

That night, I discussed the idea with Scott and we were very much in agreement that I should take part.

Soon after, I began the rigorous testing required to become a handler with Roxy. There was a 23-point test first of Roxy's behaviour, including walking her past food and making sure she could consistently and completely ignore it. Loud and sudden noises were made around her to ensure she didn't jump or bark, and balls were bounced past her. At each point, it was important that I could keep Roxy under control while the assessors made sure she wasn't displaying any strange body language. They had to be sure that no child who was already frightened of dogs would be upset by Roxy making any sudden movements.

As it turned out, Roxy was virtually bomb-proof. I was chuffed to bits when she and I passed with flying colours. We underwent full training and I learnt more about the scheme. Some of the children might have suffered an attack or bite, or picked up on a parent's fear of dogs. Occasionally they developed the fear after a dog had jumped up at them when they hadn't expected it. They were aged between three and sixteen and ranged across the spectrum in terms of how frightened they were. Some had received therapeutic help to overcome their phobia, others had spent their entire lives terrified of dogs. Our cynophobia centre was the only one of its kind in the country.

In time, we were taking part in our first class. There were four other handlers with a dog each, and a maximum of eight children. The set-up at the Essex Dog Training Centre was fascinating. There was a big main hall where all the dogs and handlers waited, and a smaller room behind it, fitted with a glass viewing panel. The children would initially enter that room with a parent or carer and look in on the rest of us. The idea was that they'd see the other children having fun with us and want to join in. If not that week, then perhaps the next.

While the children watched us, we played games with our dogs, practising agility or obedience. After twenty minutes, we'd leave the hall and go into in an adjoining room out of the children's sight. If the children wanted to, they would then come into the main hall while the instructors threw footballs around and played with them to relax them. Some of the children didn't make it to that stage on the first day.

When the main part of the class began, the children were asked to line up from one end of the hall to the other. Then we dog handlers entered with our dogs on leads. We showed the children how agile the dogs were by weaving in and out of them. Then we left the hall, swapped dogs and came back in with each other's pets. There were some squeals of delight, and even the least confident children managed a smile.

Last, we played musical mats, and the session ended with each dog lying on a mat while the children who felt able to brushed them. It was a calming way to end the session and helped the children bond with the dogs and vice versa.

As the course progressed, the tasks would become more complex and the children would have more interaction with us. I worked with children who had varying levels of cynophobia and were at different stages of the course. On average, they needed around ten hours of classes. All the way through the course, the children were repeatedly reminded that if they were frightened or needed a bit of space, they could move across the hall to where the floor tiles went grey. We told them that the handlers and the dogs would never cross that line so it was a constant safe place, should they need it.

Roxy was amazing throughout. She was very calm, and sensed when the child walking anxiously at my other side needed extra care and support while getting to know her. She didn't move suddenly or do anything unless I told her to. Her obedience was of key importance to her work with cynophobia sufferers: something as simple as Roxy suddenly turning her head to look at a child might cause meltdown.

Every week I took Roxy to work with the children. Some were violently sick with fear, and others even locked their parents out of the car so they wouldn't have to come face to face with a dog. Several froze to the spot and couldn't physically move, or sobbed, clinging to whoever they were with. I was sad to see how difficult some found being near dogs. Daniel and I had grown up with dogs and they had enriched our lives. One day, if Scott and I started a family, our children would know the love and fun dogs can bring to a home. It was a shame the children on the courses hadn't been able to share those good experiences.

Over time, the children's phobia diminished. Time and again, I saw children who initially couldn't be in the same room as a dog reward Roxy with a treat for giving them her paw. Psychologists and GPs from all over the country came to observe our work and we were sent many referrals.

In time, I repeated the training with Frank and he, too, passed the bomb-proof dog test, as I liked to call it. I was so proud of him and everything we had achieved together. He had transformed from an anxious, destructive dog, unable to find a home, to a model of good behaviour. Soon I was working with both dogs. I'd leave one in another room for half an hour while I worked with the other. Midway through the session, I'd nip out and swap them round. The kids giggled when they noticed.

I made friends with many of the families who came to us for help. One family had a ten-year-old daughter, Millie. At the end of her course, her mum said, 'It's all well and good in the class but Millie is used to the dogs here. What about when she encounters a dog somewhere outside these four walls?'

It was a valid point. We were in a controlled environment with dogs under very strict supervision. In the outside world, things were different, and we both knew it. I had a suggestion. 'Why don't I bring my dogs to your house and we can all go for a walk in the park?'

'That's a great idea,' she said.

That weekend, I put Frank and Roxy into the car and we made the twenty-minute journey to their house. When I went in, Millie was a bit nervous but much improved from the first time I'd met her. We set off to the park, and on the way there Millie held the lead of one of the dogs. But as soon as we entered the park, I sensed anxiety coursing through her. It took some coaxing but eventually she calmed down as other dogs ran about doing what dogs do, playing and sniffing.

It showed me that all the hours Roxy, Frank and I had put in had paid off because Millie was no longer overcome with crippling fear when she happened upon dogs in the course of her daily life.

The scheme continued to grow and now we have fifteen dogs and handlers at the training centre and see up to thirty-five children at a session. Parents travel for up to two hours to get to us. The scheme is not-for-profit, and we are all volunteers. I know that everyone who takes part is incredibly proud of what we continue to achieve. It's hard work and requires a lot of dedication but it's well worth it. The children feel super proud of themselves when, at the end of their course, they are handed a certificate marking their achievements.

In the summer, we typically hold a big picnic fun day and invite all the children and families who've worked with us. It's a great day out, and when I see the crowds who turn out, I'm struck by how many families can enjoy their lives together now that their child has overcome their fear.

When Frank was eight and Roxy was six, I lost my mum and it hit me hard. My family and I supported each other the best we could but sometimes only a snuggle with the dogs eased my grief. I cut back on my cynophobia work until I felt emotionally ready to go back. When I did, I noticed something that surprised me. Frank had become a bit of an old man. He tired more easily and, although he was prone to mad moments at home and during agility classes, he was slowing down.

'I think it's time to let Frank retire,' I told Scott. He agreed, then grinned at me as he realized what I was about to say. I said it anyway: 'We should think about getting another dog.'

We headed to Battersea once more and updated our details as we now lived in a bigger house. But soon after we'd put in our application, we had a surprise: I found I was pregnant. We put aside the idea of getting a new dog. After our daughter, Lexi, arrived, our house was busy. Lexi was a handful but the two dogs adored her. I knew I could trust them with her but the thought of training up a new young dog was suddenly too big a task.

When Lexi started crawling, then standing and walking, I gave the idea of a new dog some more thought. It made sense for us now to bring in a puppy that I could train from scratch and know inside out. Luckily, Scott and I were able to pick up where we'd left off with Battersea, and, one afternoon, I had a call from a rehomer. 'We've just had a litter of Staffie puppies come in, and unfortunately their mother died giving birth.'

'That's tragic,' I said. 'How are the puppies doing without their mum?'

'We've hand-reared them and they're doing well. But we thought you might want to have a look.'

Scott and I went in and we met Ronnie. As with Frank and Roxy, it was love at first sight. When we brought him home, I discovered I'd forgotten what it was like to have a puppy in the house. It had been more than a decade since Frank had chewed the door frames and pooed behind the front door! While Roxy thought Ronnie was entertaining, Frank wasn't that fussed by him. After a few days, though, I realized that it wasn't so much that Frank was disinterested in Ronnie, more that he had the hump with me! He only came to me if he needed to go outside or if he wanted food, which was unlike him because until then he had been my shadow. Now he refused to cuddle with me and took himself off to bed, or sat in the opposite corner of the room and shot me funny looks. It was as if he was saying, *Who is this mad dog, Mum? And why are you inflicting him on me?*

It was upsetting that he wasn't happy with me but how could I make Frank understand that he wasn't being replaced, that Ronnie was going to let him chill out a bit more? In time, though, he got the message and came back to me for hugs while Roxy and Ronnie chased each other like lunatics.

Lexi became good friends with Ronnie. The pair of them often watched telly together, and as Lexi was toddling around, Ronnie stuck by her to make sure she had someone to grab onto when she wobbled. It was the family life I'd always imagined for myself and Scott.

Nowadays, our brood is a happy and busy bunch. Roxy was 'head-hunted' by an animal agency who signed her for a part in a Second World War film: her agility skills were put to good use. It was challenging for us both but lots of fun too. Otherwise, my weeks are filled with Lexi, obedience training with the dogs on Tuesday, cynophobia on Wednesday, agility training on Thursday and dog shows on Saturday and Sunday. And the dogs come with me to work at school! More often than not, I'll be out with two Staffies, an English Bull Terrier and a toddler in a pram. People must think I'm mad but I wouldn't change a single thing.

Knicker Boxer Glory

The telephone at my dad's house rang and rang. It was unusual for him not to pick up so I left it half an hour and tried again. Two hours later, when he finally answered, I could hear the smile in his voice: 'Sorry, Alex,' he said. 'I was out with the dog.'

It was the brightest I'd heard him since my mum had passed away. Dad had been lonely, so my sister and I had helped him get Mickey. He'd resisted the idea of having a dog at first but we had chipped away at him, and as soon as he met Mickey he was won over. Now the two were inseparable.

'We've been out for a walk over the fields,' Dad continued, 'and now we're going to have a brew and watch some telly, aren't we, Mickey?'

In the background, there was a *woof-woof* of approval.

I'd known Mickey was the dog for Dad the minute I'd set eyes on him at a local rescue centre. He was silly and happy and bouncing in his kennel when we'd come by. He was a ray of sunshine and exactly what Dad needed. When my sister and I had driven away in our respective cars, we'd stopped at the traffic lights next to each other and I'd turned my head to see Mickey staring at me with a goofy look from her front passenger seat. I thought, He's going to be just wonderful.

For the next five years, Mickey was Dad's best friend. He was funny and often made Dad laugh. Dad taught him to get up on the footstool and when he pointed at Mickey with his hand in the shape of a gun and said, 'Bang, bang,' Mickey would fall off with his eyes shut. He'd lie stock still for a minute, then sneak a peek at his audience and ready his belly for a rub.

When Dad passed away, my sister took Mickey in, and I started thinking about a dog for my own family. My wife, Alison, and I had two children, Alex, seven, and Georgie, five. It was time for our first family pet. When I heard a friend's dog had given birth to puppies I went to see them. Even though I was a strong believer in getting a rescue dog, I reckoned a puppy was best for us as we had young kids and we could train the dog ourselves.

I arrived at my friend's house and she took me into the room where the puppies were. Seven sets of paws came thumping my way. They were Cairn Terriers, every one as beautiful as the next, and they were all set on licking me to death. How could I possibly choose one? Then the answer presented itself. The puppy who had beaten his brothers and sisters to get to me first, and subsequently got trampled by his siblings for his efforts, wriggled out from underneath them, went behind the wagging crowd and climbed onto their backs to reach up and paw me. *Pick me! Pick me!*

I brought him home and we named him Herbie. The kids loved him and he loved them in return. He was a handful, though. Herbie chewed any socks and shoes he found and, even though he had been neutered, humped anything remotely football-shaped. It was the cause of much embarrassment over the years and he never quite grew out of it. Later, whenever I took Herbie to fetch Alex after football practice, he'd find a way to slip his collar and chase the children all over the field. As soon as the shrieks of laughter went up, we all knew it was game over because Herbie wouldn't let it continue. In the summer, Herbie liked to jump into our pool over and over again, just like the kids did. Alison and I felt as if we had three children, except the third was furry, had four legs and a propensity for barking a lot.

Herbie wanted an argument with every dog he passed. Whenever we introduced him to somebody new, I'd tell them to watch their belongings around him. 'If Herbie can't make love to it, wee on it, or eat it, he tries to fight it.' That was Herbie, a real character.

Herbie was with us for thirteen years, and when he died of old age, we all felt his loss, but I felt as if my left arm had been lopped off. I worked from home, and not having Herbie to keep me company during the day, bark at anything that moved outside or come and snuggle with me while I worked was a huge blow. I felt low and depressed. All the rooms in the house were very quiet and hours would pass without a single sound besides my tapping on the computer keyboard. In a way, it was as though the life-force had disappeared from our home, as though the light had been extinguished.

We continued to contribute to the Cairn Terrier Relief Fund, and when two dogs came up that were a suitable match for us, we put our names forward. Then we realized we couldn't bring ourselves to have another Cairn. Herbie was irreplaceable. It was difficult to know what to do next, but one night Alison and I were watching *Paul O'Grady: For the Love of Dogs* on telly and a Staffie that needed rehoming came onto the screen. I said, 'If we get a rescue, let's get a Staffie.'

'We don't want a Staffie, do we?' she said, a bit anxiously. The breed had been misrepresented in the papers, which she found off-putting. Not only that: she'd need to adjust to having a bigger dog – Herbie, of course, had been quite small.

I squeezed her hand. 'Staffies just get a lot of bad press. You'll see what softies they are.'

What Alison didn't know was that I was already on the hunt for a Staffie. I had been looking at all the rescue centres in the area near our home in Sidcup, Kent, and had made a mental note to expand my search to Battersea Dogs & Cats Home. I filled in the online application form and checked on the dogs available at the home every day. Eventually I saw a dog named Barney on the website for Battersea Brands Hatch in Kent. He had big eyes and great big ears. I nudged Alex in the ribs – he was sitting next to me on the sofa. 'Let's go have a look at this one, shall we, son?' He agreed, so I called ahead to make an appointment. Monday was the earliest we'd be able to see him, which was a shame as I would be working, but Alison and Alex agreed to go. Before they set off, I said, 'If Barney is as friendly as he looks in the pictures, it's a *fait accompli* for me.'

Hours later, they were back and very excited. 'You should have seen him,' Alison said. 'He was jumping all over us. Then we took him for a walk and he was so excited about the world around him.' Alison had learnt it was likely that Barney was a Staffie Boxer cross, aged around eight or nine months old. He had the face of a bruiser and long legs. He was quite big already and simply gorgeous. They had reserved him.

Two days later, the four of us returned to Battersea to see Barney as a family. He was a bundle of energy, demanding a fuss and sitting on us at any opportunity. Battersea had little information on his background but they told us as much as they knew. He had been found as a stray wandering in Hammersmith and Fulham. I could only surmise that his previous owner had thrown him out or that he had escaped and his owner hadn't bothered to search for him. As he looked up at me with big puppy eyes, I wondered how anyone could have given up on such a lovely dog.

We brought Barney home and the whole family loved having a dog in the house again. For me, though, it brought mixed feelings. I had the dog I wanted to fill the Herbie-shaped void that had opened up after Herbie's death, but something about having another dog in the house made me think about Herbie even more than usual. Suddenly I missed him terribly and wondered if we'd made a mistake in having Barney. Seeing another dog drinking from Herbie's bowl and visiting me in the study made me wonder if I'd rushed into replacing him.

I decided to drop into Brands Hatch and talk to one of the rehomers about how I was feeling.

She was sympathetic. 'It might take some time to get used to the change.'

For a moment, I imagined not having found Barney, or coming home to find him gone: that made a new grief open inside me. Barney was such a special dog and we had barely got to know him yet. I realized the rehomer was right. We just needed to give each other time: time for me to get used to Barney and for Barney to show us the wonderful personality we knew was there.

Over the next few weeks I made a big effort to bond with Barney. Every morning at four a.m. when he woke and needed a wee, I went outside in the freezing cold and held an umbrella over both of us. He wouldn't go into the garden alone so I became his middle-of-the-night pal. He then slept on the sofa or in one of our beds – wherever his mood took him. If anyone got up to use the bathroom in the night, it was guaranteed that Barney would hijack their bed. During the day, he would run up to Alex's room and sit on his bed. It was one of his favourite spots in the house because he could look out of the window onto the main road and watch the world go by. As the days, weeks and months rolled past, it became clear that Barney was a treasure. Like Herbie before him, and Mickey with my dad, not a day went by when Barney didn't make me laugh.

He grew to a massive sixty-five pounds but he still moved about the house, and onto our laps, with his bony elbows and long legs, as if he were a fifteen-pound Yorkshire Terrier. It wasn't good enough for Barney just to be on the sofa. He wanted to be next to you, lounging against you, sitting across you. He was a big old softie. Just as I'd told Alison he would be.

Georgie always came into the house like a hurricane passing through, which would set Barney off. Either Alison or I would shout, 'Georgie, will you stop winding that dog up!' which was always followed by peals of laughter and happy barking. I loved the havoc Barney created in our home. We'd always wanted a bold dog who could deal with our many friends and visitors, and Barney was perfect for the job. He was never fazed by visitors, and had a friendly wag and a sniff ready for anyone brave enough to walk into our home.

One day I was telling some colleagues from work about my dog, and on seeing a photograph of him, a workmate said, 'Isn't that Barney from Battersea Dogs & Cats Home?'

'Yes,' I replied, with astonishment. 'How did you know?'

'They put a post about him on their Facebook page and I remember it because it made me laugh so much. He was the dog that kept eating knickers!'

That was true. When Barney had arrived at ours, he'd managed to eat every pair of pants and every odd sock he found.

Later, I logged on to Facebook and scrolled back through Battersea's posts. And there, just as my colleague had mentioned, was a picture of Barney. His gorgeous face was tilted to one side and in front of him were two pairs of black knickers. It was captioned 'The knicker-eating puppy,' and had been taken when he'd first arrived at the Home. There were nearly five thousand likes, more than thirteen hundred shares and around five hundred comments! It seemed Barney had tickled a lot of people.

'LOL, little monkey!'

'He is a cheeky one!'

'Naughty knicker nicker!'

'He looks lovely and full of mischief.'

'That's PANTS! Hope he finds a good home.'

Barney's picture had made people from all over the globe laugh and delight in his silliness. As I read through the comments, I noticed one of our neighbours had posted: 'This wonderful dog now belongs to a neighbour of mine and we see him happily going about his life now. Thank you, Battersea, for helping him when he was in need.' It was humbling to see how many fans Barney had and I felt lucky that we were his for-ever family.

Even though Barney had been quick to toilet train, he had some naughty tricks. He ripped out the many shrubs Alison had painstakingly planted around the garden and liked to dig holes under the fence to our neighbour's house. Luckily, they had a beautiful Golden Retriever, Gemma, who would go nose to nose with Barney, blocking his tunnel in. It wasn't unusual for us to go into the garden to find Gemma peering under the fence in anticipation of the defence she'd have to put up against Barney.

There were other bad habits too. He jumped up at anyone who came into the house, or whenever he got excited, which meant most minutes of every day. After a while, Alison and I called in a trainer and paid her for one-to-one obedience sessions with Barney. It was very effective when the trainer was there, as Barney was sharp when he put his mind to it. We'd watch in wonder as the trainer worked with him in the garden, telling him to sit, fetch, come, heel, stay. It was quite a sight! But the moment she left, when we tried to practise the moves and tricks she had taught us, Barney would simply stare at us, as if to say: *You two are having a laugh, aren't you? I'm not doing that!*

When the trainer wasn't around, Barney went from an attentive, smart dog to the class dunce and refused to repeat the good behaviour he'd learnt in the training sessions. Alison was very patient with him and did the bulk of his homework with him. She spent a lot of time working with him on his behaviour, and took Barney out, too, to socialize him with other dogs and people. It was then that she made a confession. 'You were right about Staffies. I had them all wrong. Barney's such a sweetheart and he really does have the softest nature.'

I was pleased he had won her round, though I always knew he would. It was a relief too that she was putting in so much time with his training. I was a bit slack and couldn't help indulging his whines for play or contact. While everyone else was out, I'd find myself talking to him: 'You're not going in that cupboard, Barney. I know what you're looking for and you're not allowed any treats.'

Barney was very nosy too. If a door was left open he'd be out like a bullet. His favourite house, other than ours, was our neighbour Kel's. If their door was open too, Barney would shoot across and race up the stairs, grabbing anything he could find, such as a towel, a teddy or a scarf, and demanding a game of tug of war. Nobody could grudge Barney a game or two. Everyone he met loved him.

Now Barney has a big fan club and he's never alone. He likes to snuggle up next to one of us and won't let us out of the door without positioning himself in the porch, ready to get into the car for whatever journey we're making – even if it's just to the station and back.

We can't imagine our life without him, and all of Alison's original doubts about having a Staffie have melted away. Best of all, my worries about replacing Herbie are long gone. Barney is everything we hoped for and more. That's why I'm such a strong believer in getting a rescue dog. There are endless reasons why a dog ends up at Battersea: it may have been abandoned, its owner may have passed away or it may have come from a loving family, who didn't want to give it up but had to. Sometimes, as in our case, a dog may have had a terrible start in life and needs – deserves – a loving home. We're biased, of course, when it comes to Barney, but anyone who meets him agrees he is smashing-looking, sweet-natured, and a lovely dog to have around. His mischievous ways make us laugh every day, and we feel very lucky to have found him.

Kobi the Great

I was just about to get into the car when my pocket began to buzz for the second time. *Ring, ring!* I was tempted to ignore it in case it was work, but when I saw the name on the screen, I answered. 'Is everything OK, Tracey?'

My wife said: 'Everything's fine, Richard. I've a large item to bring home. Do you mind coming to pick me up?'

I drove to the address she'd given me and saw her standing outside with a beautiful white Inuit dog on a lead. I recognized him as Frost, her aunt's dog. In her other hand, Tracey held a black bin-bag shaped suspiciously like Frost's bed.

Frost was a four-year-old snowy white Samoyed and he had outgrown the flat Tracey's aunt had kept him in. In honesty, we'd all been concerned about Frost for a while. He was a gorgeous dog but he needed a lot of grooming, a lot of care and loads of exercise. It seemed Tracey's aunt had reached the same conclusion and I wasn't going to argue against it. I wanted Frost.

Frost moved in permanently to our town house, where we lived with our daughter, Nicola, our son, Roo and our four cats, Berlioz, Toulouse, Charlie and Sam. The cats got a bit of a fright when we came in with Frost, but when they saw he wasn't interested in them, they settled down.

There was somebody Frost did show a keen interest in, however, and that was our mongrel, Taz. They had completely different taste in everything, from food to toys, but they were firm friends from the start. It was just as well because, for our family, dogs weren't just dogs: they were as much family as the humans in the house, so it was nice to see everyone getting along and new friendships forming.

Frost was a great addition to our family as we all led very active lives, spending our weekends and holidays camping and hiking. We loved the outdoors, and with Frost needing so much exercise, it worked perfectly. When we weren't out and about, he liked to relax in the shade on the patio. Taz, on the other hand, had been a stray that Battersea Dogs & Cats Home had picked up on the streets of London when he had been between one and two years old. They didn't know much about his background so he was a bit of a mystery. When he'd come to us, he had been frightened and anxious, using his mouth to explore everything and trying to grab our attention, but after a few days, he'd settled in and relaxed.

He loved to play-fight with Frost and they developed a special bond, but they were happy to go about their business independent of each other, too. While Frost loved being out of the house and exercising, Taz loved to be upside-down on the sofa. He was a couch potato to the core and we indulged him. Taz never joined Frost and me on our daily five a.m. walk. He'd look at us from his cosy bed as we were getting ready to go out with an expression that said, *Rather you than me!* Frost, on the other hand, couldn't get enough of it and would go for a walk come rain or shine. In rain, snow, mud, mist, fog, he was always ready and willing.

When Taz reached his seventh year, I noticed on walks with Frost that he could no longer keep up. His right hip was bothering him. As it turned out, the joint was crumbling, but a metal replacement gave him a new lease of life. Once again, our house was full of noise and chaos – just the way we liked it.

Then, in 2009, Frost seemed suddenly to stop. He was constantly tired and struggling to walk. Very quickly, he had gone from charging ahead on full power, to having a hard time doing the smallest things. He went into a rapid decline, and before we knew it, the day we had dreaded and hoped would be years away was upon us. It was inhumane to allow Frost to continue like that, so we took him to the vet. Our fears were confirmed. There was nothing more that could be done for Frost and we were heartbroken when he had to be put to sleep.

I found it hard to cope without him so we started looking around for another dog to take in. We wanted to adopt one straight away but decided to start with a foster dog to see how we'd fare, and how Taz would cope. After all, his world and the dynamic of our house had been set for a long time. In the end, we fostered a Siberian Husky.

It was a good thing we went down that road first because something strange happened. Taz, who'd always been second in command, with Frost leading the way, was now top dog and didn't want another canine in the house. We found that when we took the pair out for walks, they'd play well together. But as soon as we got back into the house, Taz began to growl at the Husky and show some behaviours that troubled us.

One night, Tracey said, 'Taz won't let the other dog at least within six feet of him.'

'He's not having any of it, is he?'

As much as it broke our hearts, we had to give up the fostering and our dream of taking in another dog, at least for the time being.

We carried on with our daily lives. Tracey's mum, Pam, and stepfather, Bernard, were both retired and lived in the basement at our home. When we were at work, they would let Taz in and out of the garden. They kept an eye on him as his beard began to go grey and when, like Frost before him, we noticed he was slowing down.

One evening, I came home from work and called him. There was no response. 'Taz!' As I opened the patio door, Mum came upstairs and said, 'I let him out a little while ago and he hasn't come back to the door yet.'

I stepped outside and found Taz curled up, asleep. It was very odd for him to fall asleep outside as he only ever went out for ten minutes at a time to do his business. But as I got closer I realized his chest wasn't moving up and down. Taz wasn't breathing. I got down on my knees and touched him. Taz had passed away. Behind me, Mum began to cry and so did I. I carried Taz inside to the lounge and we all hugged him and said our goodbyes. It was a difficult evening, very distressing for everyone as it had been so sudden and Taz was only twelve. Later, we buried him in the garden, with his favourite squeaky ball and rope toy beside him, as well as one of the neckerchiefs he liked to wear.

It was very close to Christmas but the house wasn't full of festive cheer. It felt dark, dingy and vacant. Late that night, I couldn't stop the tears flowing again. 'You're not yourself unless you have a dog,' Tracey said.

'But is it too soon for us to get another? I don't want to try to replace Taz or Frost,' I replied.

Tracey knew what I meant because that was how she felt too. But she reasoned, 'Another dog wouldn't be a replacement because Taz and Frost cannot be replaced. We just have to try to do something to make us all feel better.'

Next day, she was trawling the Battersea website while I looked at local rescue centres. We'd learnt from Frost what wonderful personalities Inuit dogs like him had and we needed a dog that had the stamina and size to keep up with our active lifestyle. No dogs we saw quite fitted what we were looking for but we left our home and drove to Battersea Brands Hatch in Kent. We reactivated our profile from when we'd taken Taz home and hoped that a suitable dog would come up.

The day after that, we decided to go to the London Home. As we went around the kennels and peered into each one, Tracey echoed what I was thinking: 'Every one of these dogs is so deserving of a home.'

But the moment I was hoping for didn't arrive, the one in which I looked at a dog, it looked back at me, and something in our hearts clicked. We talked to a rehomer and told her what we were after. She tapped on her keyboard, and every Inuit dog that came up wasn't ready for rehoming or suitable for us. One needed to live in a rural area, the other couldn't cope with cats . . .

Then, all of a sudden, I glanced out of the meeting-room window and saw a Husky being walked across the yard. 'What about that one?'

The rehomer said: 'I'll just go and find out where we're up to with him.'

When she returned, she explained that Inuit dogs typically get too stressed in the main kennels so he had been elsewhere when we'd looked around. 'This Husky was seized, with his mum and sister, a few weeks ago.'

My heart fluttered.

'The dogs have not been socialized at all, and we suspect they were very neglected and isolated. When Blue came, he weighed only eighteen kilos.' Our mouths flapped open. A Husky of Blue's size should weigh nearly double that.

The rehomer added, 'We've got him to twenty-three and he's nearly ready for rehoming.'

I couldn't help asking, 'Can we meet him today? Is that possible?'

We were shown to a meet-and-greet room, and soon the rehomer came in with Blue on a lead. He was a pure Siberian Husky with piercing blue eyes. But he couldn't make eye contact with us. He was cowering and very nervous, just a shell of a dog. It was distressing to see that majestic creature reduced to such a sorry state. Even when I offered him a treat, he wasn't sure whether or not to take it and backed off, scared. 'What has he been through to make him like this?' I said.

We were told Blue had been in a London flat with his mum, who had been used for breeding at a very early age. Along with his sister, the trio had never seen daylight and had been used as a breeding venture by their owners to make money. They had been seized by the RSPCA, then sent to Battersea for rehoming.

Tracey and I didn't need to discuss it. One look at her and I knew her emotions were in overdrive, like mine, for what Blue had been through. 'We'd love to give him a new home,' I said.

As we had cats at home, the rehomer needed to test his reaction to felines, so she left the room and returned with a big moggie in a cage. It had a cloth over it, and when the rehomer removed it, Blue stepped forward to investigate. He had a sniff and the cat stared at him, defiant. Blue was very interested but not aggressive. Then the rehomer left the room for a moment to see how Blue was with the cat when nobody had him on a lead. He settled and lay down. The rehoming team were satisfied. After much discussion, we were allowed to take him home that day, on the proviso that we would return to have him neutered when his weight was a healthy level and he was able to cope with the surgery.

Before we left, we spoke to the vet, who told us about his feeding regime and what we would need to do to get Blue to a healthy weight. He advised us to start taking Blue for walks straight away, but not to overdo it as it would take him a while to build up the stamina he should have. 'Blue has no body mass to give him energy, so keep it to thirty or forty-five minutes of walking twice a day to start.'

After our chat with the vet, we were able to load Blue into the car, along with boxes of specialist food. As soon as the doors shut, Blue scrabbled to get underneath the passenger seat. He wanted to hide, to fade into the background. It was clear he was fearful of being told off and wanted to make himself invisible.

'Whatever his previous owners did to him, they've taken every bit of dog out of him,' I said, 'and I don't care how long it takes, we're going to bring him back to life.' Tracey nodded, too moved to speak.

After a while, we began discussing his name and decided Blue was too sad, considering what he had been through in his short life. We wanted a happy name so we settled on Kobi, which was Japanese for 'joy'. It was fitting as we would endeavour to bring happiness to Kobi for the rest of his life.

Kobi was very subdued on the drive, and was still quiet when we got home, although he sniffed around and got to know his new surroundings. He kept away from the cats and they kept away from him. We had him on a long tether around the house and garden until he settled in: Siberian Huskies have a habit of jumping fences and running away.

It was a slow process to bring him back to life and he didn't even know what a ball was. It became clear to us that Kobi had never been outside and was afraid of the garden. But, with some gentle encouragement, he started to explore. Little by little, he began playing with his toys and came to show us that he loved tug ropes and soft toys. We all spent hours on the floor with him, teaching him how to play. We never told him off – we had soon found out that loud noises or shouting frightened him. Most surprising, though, was that he never barked. He was a very silent dog, and we guessed it was because he'd been told off a lot in his previous home. The only time he gave a woof was to go into the garden for a wee.

Quite quickly, he began to understand how to play but he was smart too. If I threw a ball, he'd chase it but he wouldn't bring it back. Instead he'd stare at me as if to say, *Well, I'm not your servant!*

The only problem we encountered was that Kobi was prone to tummy upsets. At first we thought it was down to stress, and then we changed his food in case that was the culprit. Nothing seemed to curb it, so we spoke to the Battersea vet, who told us to starve him for twenty-four hours, then reintroduce plain foods, such as boiled chicken and rice. He advised us to avoid treats after a bout of illness.

We did as we'd been told, but nothing helped and we were stumped. Then, one weekend, a friend came to stay and brought with him a giant bone-shaped dog biscuit for Kobi. He relished it, but later, when I went to the downstairs loo, I noticed something odd. There were biscuit crumbs on the floor, on the toilet seat and at the bottom of the loo. The truth dawned on me: Kobi had been drinking from the toilet. When I told

Tracey she was horrified. 'But we have bleach blocks in the loo!'

Even though we always put the lid down, Kobi must have pushed his snout under and lifted it. We removed the blocks, flushed every loo in the house and Kobi's digestive problems ceased. Finally, he started to put on a substantial amount of weight and we gave him lots of fresh meat, chicken and chewy treats. We discovered he loved pâté, and whenever I dared take a packet of cheese out of the fridge, he'd hear it from anywhere in the house and be in the kitchen like a shot.

In time, the outline of his ribs was covered with thick muscle. His stamina increased and our walks lengthened, then turned into runs. Whenever I got his red harness out, he knew we were about to have a proper expedition and would patiently step into it, one paw at a time. Tracey and I would ride our bikes and Kobi would lead us for ten miles without showing any signs of fatigue. He was an absolute machine.

In the summer, when it was too hot for him to run during the day, we'd go out in the middle of the night or first thing in the morning. His hind legs strengthened and his personality began to shine through. He was aloof, playful and wonderfully smart. He stopped people in their tracks with his gorgeous eyes, which were now full of emotion and intelligence. The shell we had met months earlier at Battersea had been filled with a loving, independent, fun-seeking dog.

I took my camera with me everywhere we went and snapped pictures of Kobi on woodland hikes, on the beach and scaling the snowy mountains in Wales, where we took him for camping holidays. Several times a year, we'd pack our bags, load the car and head to a working farm in North Wales. Usually, there would be between ten and thirty of us, including the kids, Nicola's boyfriend, Aarron, and my parents, Christine and Ray. We'd put Kobi on a thirty-metre running line, and let him roam around the campsite, nestled in a valley with a backdrop of mountains and hills. At night, he'd jam into our tent and sleep curled up with us in our sleeping bag, even though his breed can withstand temperatures as cold as minus fifty degrees centigrade. Kobi just wanted to be close to us at all times.

During the day, I would take him with me to scale the mountains. Tracey suffers from fibromyalgia, which meant she couldn't do the climbs, so it was just me and Kobi up in the snow. It was amazing to feel his natural instincts kick in. He'd switch from a normal run or walk into pulling mode. I was in awe of how much strength he had and felt blessed that Tracey and I had been able to help bring him back to life. He deserved every second of fun he experienced on our holidays and in our home.

Since Kobi came to stay for good, we've taken him to Mount Snowdon, the Peak District, the Lake District and every big hill in England. In time, we're going to tackle some climbs in Scotland, and we can't wait to see Kobi's face as he bounds around. We even got him a pet passport and took him on the Eurostar to visit the battlefields in Normandy.

Kobi grew very attached to me and that feeling was mutual. During the day, when I was at work, my parents took him out and we'd get email updates during the day from Mum, with a picture of Kobi. The caption would read something like: *Nan and Granddad took me to the woods today and I had lots of fun running around.* If I was away for a night, Kobi stayed in Nicola's room. She was the only acceptable overnight replacement for me! Other times, when I came downstairs with a suitcase for a work trip, he would become distressed because he knew the case meant I was going away. Nicola was the only one who brought him solace, though everybody else in the house tried! Tracey often joked that Kobi was my true soul-mate, not her.

When Nicola and Aarron announced their engagement, I joked about Kobi coming to the church as our guest of honour. After a while, it stopped being a joke. We all wanted him to be there and share in Nicola's big day. We arranged a meeting with the verger at our local church where the ceremony would be held. 'I don't suppose you'd let a dog in, would you?' I asked.

He thought about it for a moment. 'Well, I don't see why not. Kobi is one of God's creatures. I'll have to check, though.'

Two days later, we received a call telling us Kobi could come to Nicola's wedding. We were over the moon and Mum, who is a seamstress, set about measuring him up for a special suit. She bought a pattern for a smaller dog suit and Nicola's friend, who studied pattern-cutting and clothing design at university, helped to convert it to the correct size.

A couple of months later, Mum came over with the suit. Kobi stood very still and we put it on him. We all had a good giggle at how handsome our boy looked. It was a little restricted under the elbows so Mum had two further fittings until the suit was just right. He was very tolerant of it, and I reckoned it was because he was used to wearing a full harness for our walks and climbs. I did wonder, though, how Kobi would cope with the long ceremony: he isn't a very trainable dog in terms of sitting and staying. You can tell him to sit and stay but how long he actually stays put is another matter. We all agreed that if he became restless I would take him outside.

Before we knew it, the big day was upon us and I walked Nicola and Kobi down the aisle together. He almost stole the show from our beautiful bride! I handed my daughter over to Aarron and, attempting to hold back tears of fatherly pride, sat down with Kobi beside me. To my surprise, he was no trouble throughout the ceremony. Afterwards, we went outside to take photographs, Kobi smart in his bow-tie and suit. Nicola and Aarron told us that they were beginning to think they'd rather have Huskies than babies!

Little did we know that, very soon after, that dream would become reality. I'd just set off for work on a Friday morning when my mobile rang. It was my son, Roo: 'I got to the end of our road when I spotted a Husky running loose. I've got hold of him and he doesn't have a collar on.'

'I'll be right there.' I picked them both up and went to a nearby vet, who scanned him and found he had a microchip. His name was Mishka and he was four years old. The vet informed us he'd try to reach Mishka's owners and, in return, we said we'd put him up until there was any news.

Over the weekend, Mishka stole our hearts and he and Kobi got on well. Kobi was happy to have a new friend and the pair were very playful together. We quickly learnt that each dog liked a bit of space around his bowl at dinner time so we placed them a couple of metres apart. We also found that Mishka had some wily paw skills. He knew how to push door handles and open doors. It made us laugh and worry at the same time so we double-locked the outside doors when we were at home.

As the new week commenced, we made contact with Mishka's current owner through our local dog warden. It turned out the warden had come across our guest a couple of times as he had made a few escape attempts over the garden fence. Mishka's owner was at a loss about how to deal with this since a change in his personal circumstances had seen him working longer hours.

When we learnt the owner was on the verge of taking Mishka to Battersea to be rehomed, we asked to speak directly with him. 'We're happy to take Mishka in permanently,' I told him. And so Mishka became the newest member of our family. He loved cuddles and fuss, which suited Kobi. He was a little more aloof with us humans, and liked to do his own thing.

The pairing was a good one. Mishka loved to snooze on Pam and Bernard's settee, preferably with a cushion to rest his head on, but when we were out, he and Kobi ran together perfectly. The fun really began when both dogs were hooked onto my bike and decided to go in different directions around a lamppost or bollard! I made sure to watch out for those moments. Mishka was a healthy dog and able to keep up with Kobi while we were out, but on our return, he'd take a long rest on the sofa. If we disturbed him, he'd look at us as if to say: *I need a lie-down. Please leave me alone.*

Since Mishka came to stay, we've taken him on his first camping holiday to Wales. Both dogs loved it and ended up caked in mud from all the running and playing.

We can never thank Battersea enough for their kindness and dedication to their cause, which has twice given us the great privilege of sharing our life and home with a Battersea dog. Kobi had a rough start in life but now he has adventures every day. From the simple pleasures of walks in the local woods, where he can get tangled in the trees and chase squirrels, to enjoying the garden on a sunny afternoon or scaling the highest mountains in England and Wales, our boy is living the dream. Kobi doesn't waste a single minute of the new life Battersea made possible for him and we will never let him go a day without showing him how much we love him. We are honoured to help Kobi on his life of adventure.

The Road to Recovery

It was a few days after my forty-ninth birthday and I was getting dressed for work. Suddenly I caught sight of myself in the mirror. My waist had thickened and my trousers felt a bit tight. I refuse to go up a size, I thought. I'd better do something about this. 'I'm going to get fit in time for my fiftieth birthday,' I told my wife, Nina.

Nina suffered from congestive heart failure and she had a different take on life. 'You're fine as you are, Paul, but if that's what you want, you should do it.'

Once I set my mind to something, there's no stopping me. I took to jogging on my lunch break with colleagues from the Metropolitan Police, where I was a detective sergeant in child protection. The downside to working my way up the ranks was that I was no longer out and about as I had been when I was a young bobby on the beat in South London. Now my days consisted of a mountain of paperwork and managerial duties. Still, I carved time out of my day to stick to my new fitness regime, and I was pleased when, just a month later, I was already feeling better for it. In fact, it had become a part of my day I really enjoyed.

One afternoon, I was in a meeting when I started to feel a bit strange. My right arm wasn't doing what I wanted it to do and my words started coming out in a jumble. My colleague's eyes widened in horror: she'd realized I was having a stroke. I collapsed and, very quickly, an ambulance arrived to take me to hospital. A work friend got into the back of the ambulance and tried to ask me questions. I wasn't able to answer a single one. I knew that to survive a stroke I needed to receive treatment within three hours. Luckily, with the quick actions of my colleagues, I was at King's College Hospital within twenty minutes of the attack.

At the hospital, various scans and tests were conducted and I was given powerful blood thinners to disperse the bleed in my brain. Shock began to set in. I was unable to speak so I tried my best to take in the news that the bleed I'd suffered would have been fatal if I had been at home and it had hit in the middle of the night: Nina and I had separate bedrooms because of her ill health.

The next few weeks passed as a blur, and though nobody said so, I knew it was touch and go because I couldn't speak or walk. The only thing I knew for sure was that my new exercise regime hadn't brought on the stroke. It was, the doctors told me, just one of those unfortunate things in life.

Nina was unable to visit as she was so unwell, but my parents, Shirley and Alan, made the long journey from their home every day to see me.

After six weeks, I was able to return home for a few weeks. Then, luckily, I was given a place at Lewisham Hospital for intensive physiotherapy. By now I still had paralysis on my right side but I was able to walk and talk a little. Everything took three times longer to do, and often I gave up a task in a fit of rage. I felt frustrated and alone.

The following year, Nina's condition deteriorated and she was taken into St Thomas' Hospital for a few weeks. One day, when she was able to catch her breath and talk, she called me: 'Paul, I think it's best if I move to my parents' house so they can look after me.'

For many years, I had been Nina's carer but I was no longer capable of doing the job. After a while it became clear that Nina and I were unlikely to live together for the foreseeable future. It was an emotional blow for both of us, and left in tatters my resolve to recover from my stroke. The silence in my home became deafening and I became quite depressed.

Nina and I kept in touch by telephone. One day she said, 'I have a gift for you. My friend's cat has had kittens and she's agreed you can have one.'

I wasn't sure how to respond, so I kept quiet while Nina continued: 'He's a little black cat and I've named him Nino. I want you to have him so that every time you call his name, you'll remember me.'

I wanted to say so much to my wife to express my gratitude but the only words I could find were 'Thank you.'

'It will be good for you to concentrate on something outside yourself and your stroke,' Nina added.

I hoped she was right. My confidence was at an all-time low and I had come to avoid going out or talking to people because my speech was still very slow. I was embarrassed by my limitations, and with everything being so readily available online, it became quite easy to isolate myself. I ordered my food shopping on the Internet and became cocooned in my home, watching television for hours on end.

When Nino arrived, he was a breath of fresh air. He didn't judge me or look at me oddly when I couldn't get my words out, and he was good company. He didn't care that I limped when I walked or that my right hand didn't work properly any more. He just wanted love, affection and lots of cuddles.

The trouble was, Nino was an adventurer and darted out of the cat flap and into Crystal Palace Park behind my flat in South London whenever the mood took him. I couldn't relax when he was out and worried all the time about the road near our home. Then I struck upon a novel solution: a cat tracking beacon that fixed to his collar. It meant I could keep an eye on where he was with a mobile phone app from the comfort of my sofa. It was great and I learnt a lot about his habits. Nino didn't cross the road during the day when it was busy, and liked to sit by the lake in the green area behind my flat. He liked to curl up under a bush and snooze for hours. The app did wonders for my anxiety about his movements, so after six months, when I was able to return part-time to my job, I rested easy that Nino was safe.

But when it came to my job, things just weren't the same. It wasn't long before I knew in my heart of hearts that, at just fifty, my working life was over. I took medical retirement and tried to focus on building a more peaceful and slower-paced life at home with Nino. But I wasn't due any luck in that department either.

One sleepy Sunday morning, Nino had his breakfast and went out for a roam around the park. I had been watching his progress on the app and his tracker showed him in one spot by the lake. It didn't surprise me as that was a favourite place of his. But hours later, there was an urgent knock at the door. I answered it to find one of my neighbours outside with an expression on her face that I knew from my days of policing. It was the face of a person about to deliver some bad news. 'Is everything OK?' I asked, not wanting to hear the answer I knew was coming.

She took a deep breath. 'I'm so sorry, but I think Nino has been hit by a car.'

I raced outside and saw, to my horror, that she was right. We moved Nino's lifeless body from the road and I noticed his collar had come off. Later, I traced it to the spot by the lake where I'd thought he had been relaxing. It was an awful day. I didn't know what I'd do without my cat.

The next few months were difficult, and it seemed that, no matter how much I battled on, obstacles were placed in front of me. Eventually I suffered a nervous breakdown, and spent three months living with my parents and recovering.

As the New Year arrived, I made a decision. I contacted local cat rescues. Nino had brought me so much joy and I reckoned a new cat would begin what I hoped would be an upward curve in my life. But when each organization learnt about how Nino had died, they refused me as an applicant. It was understandable, given the risk the busy road outside my house posed, but I was in despair about where to turn to next. I didn't have it in me to pack up all my things and move to a new home. I had seen enough change in my life without putting myself through such a big upheaval.

It was then that I began thinking about Battersea Dogs & Cats Home. When I had been a young uniformed officer at Southwark police station, we'd often had to pick up stray and lost dogs and keep them in our kennels until an owner showed up or Battersea were able to collect the animal for rehoming. But while the dogs were with us, I fed and walked them. Every now and again, I would form a special bond with a particular dog and decide to take it home for myself and Nina. This was many years before microchipping so it was impossible to track an owner if they didn't come forward. Over the years, Nina – who loved animals as much as I did – and I had adopted six dogs and taken much joy from them in the earlier years of our marriage. They each stayed with us, leading happy and fulfilled lives, till they died of old age.

Now, as I thought about getting another cat, I decided Battersea would be my next port of call. For many years, I'd thought of myself as a secret Battersea ambassador, so this time it made sense to give them a ring. I wondered if perhaps an older cat that wanted to stay inside would work for me and I hoped Battersea could find a responsible way for me to have one.

When I spoke to them on the phone, the adviser was very friendly, helpful and patient with me as I tried to get my words out. She invited me to come down for a proper chat, so the next day I took the train to the Home. I spoke with a rehomer there, and when she discovered I'd kept dogs for many years, she said, 'Why don't you pop up and see the dogs we have in at the moment?'

It hadn't occurred to me to have a dog, with all their physical needs, and I didn't want to rush into anything simply because I was so lonely. 'I'm not sure,' I said. 'Can I think about it?'

'Of course. Take all the time you need. We'll be here when you're ready.'

I thought about it for a couple of weeks and decided that, actually, a dog was probably better for me than a cat. A dog would give me the company I craved, and it would get me out of the house more than a cat would because it would need walking every day, regardless of the weather.

Recently my recovery from the stroke had plateaued. I wasn't getting out of the house enough, even though I lived next door to a beautiful park. I was trying to take short jogs through it but that wasn't a sociable hobby. A chapter of my life had closed: I wasn't working, my wife and I were no longer living together, and I wasn't socializing at all. Communication was still difficult for me and I had let that narrow my world to the four walls of my home.

Maybe it was time for a big change.

I began looking through the dogs available on the Battersea website and saw there was an abundance of Staffies. A brindle-coloured female caught my eye so I went in, hoping to meet her. When I talked to a rehomer, I was told that that particular dog had a number of complex problems and, given my health, we weren't a good match. The second dog I hoped to see was possessive, better placed with a family than an individual. Then the rehomer said, 'I have a timid girl called Bibi and I think she would be just right for you. Would you like to meet her?'

'Yes, please, but can you tell me more about her first?

Bibi, a Staffie, had been brought in with her latest litter of puppies several months earlier. While they had all been rehomed quick as a flash, she had been left behind, sad and pining for her pups. She had become increasingly introverted and unhappy.

I was taken to a meeting room and took a seat while the rehomer went to fetch Bibi, who was two and a half years old. When the rehomer brought her in, I saw she had a beautiful black coat and soft, gentle eyes. But she seemed as down in the dumps as I felt and wouldn't make eye contact. She didn't even have the curiosity in her that I would have expected from any dog that comes into a new room. She didn't sniff around to see what was what, and wouldn't leave the rehomer's side. When we were left alone together, she kept her head and tail down. I slowly moved towards her and held out my hand with some treats. She tentatively reached forward and had a few. She perked up a little bit, just enough to look me in the eye. In that moment, something clicked between us. It seemed that Bibi needed me as much as I needed her.

I decided to take a day to think about it, even though, deep down, I knew she was meant to be mine. 'Can I reserve her and think about things overnight?' I asked the rehomer. 'I'm very interested in her but I want to be quite sure.'

'Yes,' she said. 'That's a good idea.'

We filled out the relevant paperwork and I returned home to think long and hard about the commitment I'd be making to a young dog like Bibi. As the hours wore on, I realized I didn't feel daunted but excited. Tonight may be the last night, I thought, that I'll be alone in this flat.

The next day, I returned to Battersea to collect Bibi for good. I had one question for them, so a vet from the clinic came to answer it for me. I wanted to know if Bibi's undercarriage, which was drooping from having a number of large litters, would ever recover. 'I'd hate people to think I'd been the one to breed from her so irresponsibly.'

'It might bounce back because she's still relatively young,' the vet said, 'but in many cases this kind of damage doesn't improve.'

I accepted that Bibi's body might never recover from what she had been through, and if people were going to judge me as being responsible for the state of it, then I'd just have to live with it. After all, if they ever stopped to talk to me, or get to know us, they'd find out she was a rescue dog.

I also learnt that when Bibi had come to Battersea with her two puppies, aged eight weeks, she had been terrified of people and had sat in her bed trembling or cowering. The staff had described her as 'shut down'. I found that incredibly sad. It wasn't just emotional problems: Bibi had been neglected physically too. She was underweight at 16.6 kilos, her ears were dirty and her fur was thinning, which had revealed old scarring to her head and fore limbs. She'd had a terrible start, and I was determined to give her a good life.

I took Bibi home on the train and she was very nervous on the journey. I made a mental note to try to drive rather than use public transport as it was clear the escalators freaked her out.

When we arrived home, Bibi wouldn't leave my side and was very timid. She had a few accidents on the carpet and cowered while I cleaned them up. It made me think that perhaps in the past she'd been told off harshly or smacked for that sort of thing. When I'd finished, I spent a while petting Bibi and talking to her softly. I hoped in time she'd decide I wasn't a danger to her and realize I would always be kind to her, even if she did have an accident in the house.

Although Bibi was wary of me, she wanted to be near me all the time. That night, she followed me into the bedroom, ignoring her own bed, and slept on the end of mine. For the first time in months, I felt a glow of happiness. I knew then that she and I would become very dear to each other.

Next day, I clicked on Bibi's blue Battersea lead and we stepped outside together. That first walk felt symbolic in a lot of ways: a new start for both of us. I took her across the road to the park and I was no longer the lonely man who had suffered a stroke and now wobbled about. I was just a normal man and his dog, taking a springtime walk in the park and getting some fresh air. I had a purpose and I found myself standing a bit taller, feeling less self-conscious of my body and the way it moved. I revelled in this new experience.

Within a matter of weeks, we had built up to four walks a day. Bibi was becoming much more comfortable with me too, but at first when I let her extender lead loose, she chose to stick beside me rather than run ahead. As the weeks passed, she grew in confidence. She went further ahead of me and explored more. She was starting to behave like a curious dog, as she should, rather than the poor creature I had first met.

I learnt that Bibi had great recall and spent a lot of time reinforcing that with treats, ahead of letting her off the lead. When the time was right, I knelt down, unclicked Bibi's lead, and before I'd had time to get on my feet again, she had shot off, running at full pelt across the grass towards the car park. I raced after her in a panic that she might get hit by a car. Then I realized that Bibi thought we were playing so I stopped, which prompted her to run excitedly back to me. I laughed as I looked over my shoulder and registered how far I had sprinted. I hadn't run so far or so fast since before the stroke. It felt good to throw caution to the wind and do what I wanted to do without wondering first if my body could handle it. My doctors had been reassuring me for some time that it was fine for me to exercise and I had been gingerly taking short jogs but I was always worried. Now my concern for Bibi had forced me to run after her as fast as I could.

As our daily walks increased in length, I felt two things in my body change. Since the stroke, my right leg had been out of sync with the rest of my body, but all the walking and running after Bibi was getting my body and brain talking to each other again. I also found that my chronic fatigue, a side-effect of the stroke, was much improved. Before Bibi, I had needed a number of naps through the day, and there were still days when I needed them but I was improving and could do more than I had in a long time.

There was a change in Bibi's body too. Her belly was no longer hanging down near the ground, and there was some definition in the arch of muscle that ran from her midriff to her back legs. I was pleased to see that she was getting as much out of our walks as I was.

After her bolt across the park when I had let her off the lead for the first time, she was great when she was free and I had her on a lead only when we were near a busy road. And that was simply because I felt a bit nervous. I came to accept that she'd never step away from me when it was busy.

As the hours we spent outside the house increased, so did my social interaction with other people. There was a large community of dog walkers and they were very friendly. We all stopped to chat when we saw each other, and as the dogs made friends with one another, I made new friends, too. My speech came on in leaps and bounds because I was speaking frequently once more. Before Bibi, days and days would pass when I wouldn't see a soul or utter a single word. Now not a day went by when I didn't bump into a familiar face and have a conversation. Better yet, I found myself arranging trips to the pub or another park with fellow dog walkers. It was an amazing turnaround for me and in such a short space of time.

With my new friends, I went along to the weekly pub quiz at our local. Bibi came too and sat quite comfortably under my chair. I felt happy. I was out and about, I had new friends, I had a social life – all things I'd thought would be impossible before Bibi came into my life. It got me thinking about what else I really wanted that I'd ruled out as impossible since the stroke. I looked into trips away from London and decided on a camping holiday to Canterbury. It was the first holiday I'd been on since the stroke, and before I'd got Bibi I wouldn't have dreamt I was capable of it. The progress I'd made with her around was amazing.

At the end of August, I packed a bag, loaded the car and set off with Bibi. She was so good in the car: she curled up on the front seat and slept all the way there. Just having her next to me made me feel calm and able to complete the journey, something else I wouldn't have allowed myself to wish for before her.

The weather at that time of the year should have been balmy but it turned out to be rainy and cool. Bibi and I went for long walks by the canals, stopping at a country pub when we felt like it. Everywhere we went, people stopped to talk to me about her. They could soon see what a wonderful dog she was and many remarked on how she never stopped staring at me. It seemed clear that she was as infatuated with me as I was with her. We wiled away the hours with new friends, and every night in the tent, she made me smile by hogging the sleeping bag. I was happy to let her have most of it because it made me happy to look after someone else.

I thought a lot about Nina on that trip. I couldn't take care of my wife like I used to, but at least with Bibi in my life, I was doing something productive with my days. It was bittersweet to realize that I'd replaced my relationship with my wife with the one I now had with Bibi.

Some weeks later, when I said this to Nina on the phone, she said, 'Paul, I just want you to be happy. However that comes to you, it makes me happy too. Maybe sometime soon I can meet Bibi.'

'I'd love that,' I said.

Just as Nina looked out for my emotional well-being, even from far away, Bibi did the same but much closer. She followed me around and it became clear to me that she was a very empathetic dog. She seemed to sense when I was upset, or when frustration at my broken body got the better of me. Sometimes I wasn't able to use my hands properly and Bibi would sit beside me until I'd finished having a strop and completed my task. She could always calm me down and I hoped I could harness that feel-good factor for Nina too.

It took some time to convince Nina's parents that it was a wise idea for me to take Bibi to meet her: they were worried a dog would be too boisterous around Nina and stress her, but I knew Bibi would do me proud. I drove her to see Nina and she hopped on the bed, sniffed Nina and promptly shut her eyes for a nap. It was a special moment for me to see Nina smile and glow again.

Later, I took Bibi on another holiday, this time a canal-boat trip for four days. We rode up and down the waters near Leighton Buzzard. Bibi didn't like staying on the boat without me, so if I had to get off for any reason, she'd follow me. Apart from that, she coped well with the trip. Maybe one day, I thought, I'd sell up and buy a canal boat to live on with Bibi. Without the new confidence she had given me, I would never have considered exploring that pipe dream of mine.

It's been a few years now since my stroke, and when I look in the mirror, I finally feel as though this difficult chapter of my life is closing. I might never be the person I was before the attack, but I have rediscovered myself, as well as finding out new things that I like and want to do. I credit most of my progress through this phase of my life to Bibi. She got me out into the world again and pushed me gently to do things for her sake that I would have put off doing for myself. An awakening of sorts.

I know now, having lived through a stroke, that the prospect of recovery can be very daunting. I know how easy it can be to give up: to give up on talking to people when words escape you or your memory fails you; to give up on going out because walking is beyond your physical capability; to give up on opening that can of soup because your hand won't listen to what your brain is telling it to do. My advice to anyone who finds themselves recovering from a stroke or other serious physical ailment is: please don't give up hope because that's the worst thing you can do. Instead, put some energy into something outside yourself. For me, that thing was Bibi. Bibi is faithful, loyal and caring. I couldn't have asked Battersea for a better match for me.

You can do no better in this life than accept the unconditional love of a dog.

The Three Musketeers

I'd just finished a long shift at the hospital and I was exhausted. My feet were throbbing and I had a head-ache, the kind that starts behind your eyes and creeps over your skull. The thought of cooking dinner was too much, so on the way home, I stopped at the shop and bought steak and onion pies for my husband, Dave, and my son, Jason.

When I got in, our Doberman, Kimmy, and Lurcher Labrador cross, Shadow, were waiting by the door for me. They jumped around excitedly so I placed the pies at the back of the kitchen worktop while I said hello. The girls were my welcoming committee, and not a day went by when I came in from work and they didn't dance around me.

After a few minutes of cuddles, I told them, 'Now, you two, I'm popping up to get changed. Behave your-selves for five minutes and I'll come down and give you your dinner.'

They looked at me as if butter wouldn't melt, their tails swishing from side to side in unison.

I went upstairs, kicked off my nurse's uniform and pulled on some jogging bottoms and a sweater. But when I came back downstairs, I heard a suspicious crunching. *Oh, no . . .* As I rounded the corner, I saw that Shadow and Kimmy were crammed into one bed, each with a pie in her mouth. Kimmy looked at me – *What? What have I done?* I knew she was far too timid to have instigated the theft. As always, Shadow was the mastermind behind Pie-gate. I could imagine how it had panned out. The moment I'd turned my back, Shadow would have had her paws on the worktop, scuffling to get close to the pies. She would have jumped and jumped and jumped until she'd got her chops around one. Then she would have taken it to Kimmy, who, of course, wouldn't have turned down such a delicious treat. When Kimmy was all sorted, Shadow would have returned for pie number two. The perfect crime, if only they had scoffed them quicker.

I couldn't stay mad at the pair because I loved them so much. So, off I went, back to the shop to buy dinner all over again.

And that was what life was like for Dave and my children, Jason and Jordan, and Dave's children, Elysia, Joseph and Grace, with our dogs around.

We were mad about dogs and had always had them in our lives, mostly rescues. We loved Battersea Dogs & Cats Home because the work they did for animals was tremendous. Battersea shared Dave's and my passion for animals and were as committed to finding them the right homes, and vetting potential candidates properly, as we were to ensuring the animals in our care thrived.

Shadow and Kimmy were both rescues. Kimmy was a pure-bred Doberman and our first family dog. Some years later, I'd come home one day to find Shadow prancing about in the kitchen. Dave had taken her in from the local dog rescue near our home in Crowthorne, Berkshire. From that moment, Kimmy and Shadow had been as thick as thieves, quite literally, chasing each other in the garden, then curling up together in one bed, on the sofa or by the radiator.

Then, when Kimmy was twelve, she started to go off her food. Shadow was also turning her nose up at dinner time so I reckoned they had both picked up a stomach bug. But when Kimmy started whining in the night, I knew something was wrong. Kimmy never barked or made a sound so that whining worried me. As a nurse, I knew that pain in the night was not good news. I also noticed she was drinking a lot of water but wasn't going out to wee any more than usual. As we got ready for bed one night, I told Dave, 'I think Kimmy's kidneys are failing.'

He looked as heartbroken as I felt. 'What shall we do, Christine?'

Kimmy showed us the answer: the next morning, she couldn't get up. I called the vet to make an appointment. Then Jason wrapped Kimmy in a blanket, lifted her into his arms and headed towards the car. Shadow, who was always showboating about the house with her gorgeous long legs and usually simmering with energy, stood with her tail between her legs and let out a cry. She knew as well as we did that Kimmy wasn't coming back. It was heart-breaking, and I cried as we drove to the veterinary clinic, knowing what was about to happen.

Dave met us there from work. As the vet explained that Kimmy's kidneys were indeed failing, and the kindest thing would be to put her to sleep, I took Dave's arm. 'I can't be here.'

I kissed Kimmy goodbye and left the room, wishing I could take her home with me and nurse her until she slipped away. But that wouldn't have been the right thing for Kimmy, only for me.

Some time later, the boys came out with red eyes and I knew she was gone.

When we got home, Shadow wove in and out of our legs, looking for Kimmy. When she realized Kimmy hadn't come back, she began to whine. Her best friend was gone and she knew it. The vet had told us to try to remain positive around Shadow, as she would pick up on our sadness and Kimmy's loss would be even harder for her to deal with. We had to do our best to support her as we all grieved together.

Without Kimmy, the house seemed horribly empty. Shadow stuck to us like glue and it was having her in such constant and close proximity to me that made

Her Majesty the Queen officially opened the new kennels.

When Irene's husband John (top left) lost his battle with cancer, it was her daughter Ali (top right) who suggested she go to Battersea.

Irene fell in love with Grace, a Norwegian Forest Cat, who in turn nursed Irene back to happiness.

English Bull Terrier Roxy and Staffie Frank are two rescue dogs who became firm friends!

Despite initially showing behavioural problems, Frank's owner took him to obedience classes and he went on to become a star agility and therapy dog.

Husky Kobi became a central part of his adoptive family, even playing a starring role at a wedding!

Before being rescued, Kobi had never seen sunlight. Now, he can't get enough of the great outdoors.

Barney the stray Boxer-Staffie puppy, who had mysteriously
digested three pairs of knickers!

Bibi the Staffie, who helped rehabilitate her new owner after he had
suffered a stroke.

Bailey the Lurcher joined three other rescue dogs for a new life in France.

Bubbles the American Bulldog with best friend Duke.

Leila the Jack Russell helped her owner to cope with clinical depression.

In turn, Leila overcame her timid nature to become a cheeky and sociable pet.

Just some of the many pets cared for by Battersea Dogs & Cats Home.

me notice her doing something strange. 'Dave, have you noticed Shadow won't go through doorways any more?'

He nodded. 'It took me ten minutes to get her out of the front door yesterday for a walk.'

Then it dawned on us. Shadow must have thought Kimmy had disappeared when she'd gone through a door, and if Shadow did the same she might not come back.

We gave Shadow lots of love and attention, and often went through doorways with her in our arms, to repeat the journey in reverse five minutes later in the hope she'd understand that she was quite safe.

Shadow was five when we'd taken her in but we were ready to give her all the love and care she needed. When she'd arrived, she surprised us by teaching Kimmy how to play and walk together. Kimmy had been mistreated before she arrived with us, and when Shadow had come along, she'd shown Kimmy how to roll around in the mud and, in a lot of ways, how to be a dog. She had been dynamic and playful and the two of them had shared lots of special times together.

It was no surprise to us that Shadow was pining for her playmate. As the weeks dragged on, she didn't show any improvement. And, to be honest, neither did we, so we decided to get another dog to keep Shadow company. Hopefully, it would brighten us up too. We returned to the rescue centre Shadow had come from.

There, we told the lady what had happened to Kimmy and that we'd like a companion for Shadow.

'Are you looking for a male or a female?' she asked.

'It doesn't matter as long as the two of them get on well.'

The lady went to the kennels and returned with a beautiful brindle-coloured Lurcher, a Greyhound Saluki cross. He was prancing about just like Shadow always did. They had a bark and a sniff of each other and then we set off on a walk. The two dogs strutted along happily together and clearly got on, so we took him home and named him Mars.

For the first few hours, Mars ran excitedly all over the house, upstairs, downstairs, into the kitchen, behind the sofa, into the garden, exploring every nook and cranny in a flurry of excitement. When he finally calmed down, he jumped onto the sofa and that was it. He lay back, legs akimbo, with an expression on his face that said, *This is my place now and this is where I'm staying.* If we tried to move him, Mars was very clear: *Talk to the paw because the face isn't listening.* Shadow didn't follow him around, but her tail was wagging as she watched the little nutter that had entered our home.

After a couple of weeks, Shadow and Mars were inseparable, and she was doing to him what she had done with Kimmy for all those years. She gently tugged at his legs to get him onto his feet: *Come and play with me instead of sitting there!* Now, instead of Shadow chasing Kimmy around the garden, it was

Mars chasing Shadow. They were a great match as playmates, and whenever Shadow hesitated at a doorway, Mars coaxed her through. It was wonderful to see their bond developing. And Mars was a gentleman: he waited for Shadow if she dawdled on a walk and would graciously hand over a treat or a toy if she bugged him for it. I often joked to Dave, 'If only Mars was a human, he would be the perfect man!'

A year passed and my birthday was coming up. One day I was reading the *Bracknell News* when I spotted a pull-out section, advertising dogs available for rehoming from Battersea Dogs & Cats Home. The centre nearest us was Old Windsor and they had a beautiful Lurcher pictured, ready for adoption. I showed the picture to Dave. 'Let's give Battersea a ring,' he said.

I was disappointed when I heard the Lurcher had already been rehomed, but the lady said, 'Have a look on our website. We have a number of similar dogs available.'

I began a new search, and as I browsed through the gallery, there was one dog I kept coming back to. He was a Lurcher named Snow, and he'd been taken to Battersea on Boxing Day, weighing just nineteen kilos. He was severely emaciated and had been found wandering around Wraysbury, Surrey. The working theory was that Snow had been kept by travellers for coursing, going down into holes and pulling out hares and rabbits for food. Snow, who was just shy of four years old, had pressure sores and scars on his legs. It was likely he had been left to lie on hard floors for most of his life. I knew I had to see him.

I called the Home and, luckily, Snow was still available. He had been with a foster-mother but she was due to have an operation so he was now back in the kennels and very much in need of a permanent home. I knew I had to see him. 'Can we come and meet him?'

'Yes,' the rehomer said. 'Please bring your dogs with you so they can all have a meet and greet.'

Next day, we went along to see Snow. We were shown into a meeting room where he was lying quietly on his bed. He didn't lift his head but his eyes followed us. He was in a pitiful state and I could tell by his demeanour that he'd had a horrible time before he'd been brought into Battersea by a member of the public. His eyes were sad and it was clear he was suffering from depression. My heart went out to him. I sat with him and he let me stroke his head but it seemed like the first time he'd been touched with kindness. He didn't understand what anything was and didn't realize he could eat treats, or even that he was allowed to. After a while, Dave returned home to fetch our dogs, and we were taken to an enclosed area where all three dogs could be let off their leads. Mars and Shadow rushed over to Snow, excited to meet him. They wanted to play with him. Unfortunately, given his delicate state, Snow was overwhelmed and cowered away from them, backing into a corner with his tail between his legs. Mars and Shadow didn't understand

and kept trying to play. Emma, the rehomer, stepped in: 'I don't think this is going to work, I'm afraid.'

I could appreciate her concern, but Dave and I knew our dogs inside out. They weren't a threat to Snow: they wanted to befriend him. 'They'll be fine, I know they will. They're just excited to meet a new friend.' Emma wasn't convinced but then I had an idea. 'Can we come back tomorrow and try again?' I reckoned that, now our two had met Snow, they would be a bit calmer and show Emma that the three of them could get on well together as a little trio.

The next day we returned and I hoped that everything would go smoothly. This time, I let the dogs off their leads in the room and they wandered around calmly, had a sniff and that was it. They didn't try to play with Snow or each other, and sat down quietly next to Dave and me.

We had a long chat with Emma, and though she was still concerned about how the dogs had reacted the day before, I reassured her that we were experienced owners and Dave and I, as well as the kids, would be around to police the three until they got used to each other. Eventually, we decided to go ahead with the adoption, and were over the moon to be able to take Snow home that day. We renamed him Bailey and started the process of getting the three dogs used to each other.

We kept them apart with baby gates to begin with, to let Bailey settle into our home. Mars and Shadow were fine about the new dog in the house, however, and generally let Bailey be. On the first day, he was still a little nervous and it was clear he felt a bit out of place. While Mars and Shadow slept in one bed together, Bailey was happy to stay in his own on his side of the fence. When Mars and Shadow ran into the kitchen for their dinner, Bailey ran in with them and looked at them, as if to ask, *What's happening, guys? Why are we running?* They were very patient with him, and if he ate from their bowls, they didn't grumble.

After a couple of weeks, we let Bailey into the garden with one other dog at a time. I watched him closely and saw that he was copying what his play-mate was doing. It was clear that Bailey was following Shadow and Mars's lead and it was heart-warming to see the special connection forming between the trio. Occasionally, he and Mars had a play-fight, and while their tales were still wagging, we let them play. If it got any more serious we were ready to separate them, though it never came to that. While we all took care of Bailey's needs, we were careful to give Mars and Shadow lots of attention too, to stop them growing resentful of the latest addition to the family.

The kids came to visit often, and one day Jason came in with a baseball cap on. For the first time in weeks, Bailey started cowering. When Jason took his cap off, Bailey was fine once more. We reckoned he hadn't recognized Jason and that was why he'd freaked out. But when my friend came over wearing a cap,

Bailey reacted negatively again. We grasped that he was fearful of men in caps or hats so we alerted any friends or relatives coming over to avoid covering their heads. It was sad to see Bailey's reaction in situations like that, and I wondered what he had been put through to cause that behaviour.

As time passed, Bailey's weight gradually increased until he was up to an acceptable thirty-three kilos. With the long walks and the many hours the three dogs spent playing in the garden, his muscles had become firm and toned, and his pressure sores had disappeared – I had bought him the softest padded bed I could find. He was becoming the picture of health, just like his new brother and sister.

Gradually Bailey came out of his shell and showed his true personality. He loved to follow me around, and if I was in the house, he stayed by my side for company. But if the others were in the garden, he ran outside to chase them, destroy my potted plants and roll in any fox poo he could find. He was quite easy to influence, and if Mars and Shadow got into trouble, I knew Bailey wouldn't be far behind, wreaking some other havoc. But I wouldn't have changed the chaos for anything. Our house was hectic, full of noise and laughter. It felt alive. Soon, Mars, Shadow and Bailey all crammed into one bed together for naps so we began to call them the Three Musketeers.

In time, Dave and I made a life-changing decision. He had worked as a mechanic for British

Airways for many years, but as he was getting older, he was finding the physical work more and more difficult. When the opportunity came up for him to take voluntary redundancy, we had a long chat about it.

'If I take it,' Dave said, 'we'd be able to move to France like we've always dreamt of doing.'

'That's scary and exciting all at once,' I said.

After much deliberation, we decided to take the plunge. We'd spent many holidays and summers with the kids in France, and now that they were all grown-up and had moved out, it was the perfect time for us to make our retirement dreams a reality. We loved the little villages in the south, the pace of life and the life-style that living there would afford us.

In the new year, we went over to look at some properties. One instantly stole our hearts. It was two hundred years old and set in an acre of grounds. It was built around an old forge, which had been used to make cannon balls in the Napoleonic wars, as well as the actual steel used in King Henry VII's sword. The Queen Mother had even been to stay there in the sixties. The house itself had seven bedrooms, the same number of bathrooms, and two gatehouses where the main gates met. The rest of the land was enclosed with really high walls, making it very safe for the dogs. As we walked around, I pictured the dogs running free in the grounds and having the time of their lives. The back door opened on to a manicured garden, which backed onto a river. That day, we put in an offer. It was accepted.

A few months later, we packed up our belongings and moved to Feuillade, in south-west France, with our Three Musketeers. It felt fitting that our trio were now about to embark on a wonderful life in France, following in the footsteps of their group's namesake.

My stepfather, Alan, helped Dave put a gate at the bottom of the back garden to prevent a dog running off and falling into the river, so our home and our land were now secure for them. We left the kitchen door open and they raced in and out all day long to their hearts' content.

But Bailey was the one who made our emotions bubble over. Every morning, he'd get up, head outside and run like the wind, his ears flat against his head. I was moved to tears of happiness more often than I'd care to admit. It was hard to believe this was the dog that hadn't been able to lift his head to look at us and had cowered when his comrades wanted to play with him. I knew Dave felt as I did, and we were so grateful to have been able to give Bailey this fresh start.

As time went on, Bailey learnt how to truly enjoy life as a dog and, most of all, to earn some treats. He learnt to sit on command, give his paw and roll on to his back. His friends did a good job of teaching him something else too. He knew that when I said, '*Who* . . .' it was time to come running. I rarely had to finish the sentence, 'Who wants a treat?' before all three had raced into the kitchen and were waiting near the treats jar.

Life in France was blissful, and we loved having the children with us. One summer, Jordan and his girlfriend, Carmen, came to visit and we were walking around our land when Mars came up to us and started getting under our feet. 'Mars, go back to the house,' I said. Usually, he would oblige my requests but this time he wouldn't leave us alone. 'Mars, stop being a naughty boy. Go back to the house.'

But he would only go as far as the forge, then run back to us. He did this loop over and over, and when I ignored him, he ran to the forge, and back to Jordan, barking as he went.

By now, we weren't so much annoyed as intrigued. 'I'll go and see what he wants,' Jordan said. He disappeared with Mars, and a few minutes later, they were running towards me. 'Mum, Shadow's stuck on the other side of the river.'

I'd no idea how she'd got out of our grounds, but reckoned she'd been chasing a river rat.

Now we were all running. Carmen took Mars back to the house to fetch Dave while Jordan and I went to where he'd seen Shadow. There she was, on the other side, looking rather alarmed. She kept glancing at the moving water and back at us. *How am I going to get back to you?*

Jordan got into the canoe we kept by the river. 'If I push across in this, I should be able to haul her in and bring her back.' As Jordan made his way across, Shadow jumped into the water and began paddling across to him. But as she began to tire, her head kept disappearing under the surface. Meanwhile, I was yelling, 'Grab her collar, Jordan, pull her in!' Eventually, Jordan caught hold of it and, with some hard pulling, got her on board and back to safety.

Jordan was in tears and so was I. We'd both thought she was going to drown. If it hadn't been for Mars alerting us to his friend being stranded, she might well have died.

As we settled into life in France, we decided to take in another dog. We had the space and time for it and, really, there wasn't any good reason not to! We got in touch with SPA – Société Protectrice des Animaux – a French dog rescue organization, and met Galopin, a four-year-old Labrador. He had been in the kennels for two years and nobody could understand why he hadn't yet been lucky enough to find a for-ever home. He was a lovely dog with a fun personality and we reckoned he would fit in well with our three. When they met, they all sniffed each other and quickly began to play. He made friends with our Musketeers, no problem, and paired up with Bailey. That made Mars a bit jealous and, occasionally, he would have a growl. It was to be expected as our threesome became a foursome and got used to each other.

It served us well having four dogs, because when we went out to the local village to do some shopping or run some errands, the Three Musketeers kept Galopin busy. He became nervous when we went out and would chew anything he could get his paws on – cushions, pots and pans out of the sink, even the stuffing from the sofa.

It's still early days with Galopin and we're doing some training with him. The teething problems he's experiencing aren't unexpected in a rescue dog but we're the couple to give him the time and dedication he needs. We firmly believe that rescue dogs are worthy of a second chance in life.

All our rescues have brought so much to our lives and our family. If you've got room in your home and in your heart, and are prepared to give a dog time and patience, then a rescue dog should be at the top of your list. All of my favourite family times and memories are highlighted by the presence of our dogs, and they are memories I will cherish for ever.

Some of the toughest times we've experienced as a family have been eased by our dogs. If you're feeling down and want the world to leave you alone, a dog won't intrude on that. It will sit with you and make sure you're all right without asking for anything in return. They simply love you without question and that's what we will do in return for the rest of their lives.

The Best Therapy

I shut the door to the living room and climbed the stairs with what felt like the weight of the world on my shoulders. I was eighteen and had just told my father something life-changing – that I was gay. He was a hardened military man and didn't take the news in his stride. In fact, he told me to pack my bags and get out of the house.

We'd had blazing rows in the past about religion and where I wanted to take my life but we'd somehow muddled through with our differing views, locking horns and getting over it. But this time was different and we both knew it, so I did as Dad asked. I packed a small duffel bag with essentials and took the first train to London, far away from my hometown of Forres.

Somehow, I found my feet and made new friends from all walks of life. I joined a Hare Krishna temple and spent much time in a monastery in central London. Many years passed and my circumstances changed from year to year, but one thing remained the same: there seemed to be a hole inside me that, no matter how much I prayed, or wished or pleaded, was never filled. I lost my faith and felt more alone than I ever had.

I bit the bullet and wrote to my mother, who was now stationed in Belgium with my father, and in return, she sent me a one-way ticket to join them. When I arrived, Dad laid down some very clear ground rules about relationships while I was on the base and we agreed that nothing would go on in his house. But I wasn't interested in physical relationships because I was searching for something to counter my loneliness – true companionship, which I had lacked all my life

Some days, my pain was so unbearable that I no longer wanted to be around. I made several suicide attempts, and eventually sought help. I began psycho-therapy and was diagnosed with clinical depression, as well as seasonal depression, which came on in the winter months. Once I understood this, the seemingly inexplicable dark episodes I'd suffered throughout my life started to make sense. Medication helped but it wasn't quite enough.

I returned to London and tried to get on with my life. I rejoined the temple and took a job. After some years, I began volunteer work in the community, found a partner and we settled down to living our lives together. I still suffered very dark periods but I felt better for knowing that I had someone special in my life who loved me, no matter what. He was a great support to me.

One January, I started experiencing night sweats, headaches and flu symptoms. I had a niggling feeling that I knew what might be causing it, having seen friends suffer the same fate. I went to the doctor, who ordered a series of blood tests. One was positive and I returned to see a health adviser to hear which it was. She sat me down and said, 'I'm sorry to tell you, Barney, that you've tested positive for HIV.'

My suspicion had been correct. The health adviser was very comforting, but I could tell she was expecting me to break down or express fear and anxiety. Instead I was surprisingly calm. I think I was in shock. I listened to everything she needed to tell me about my treatment plan and then took some time to try to come to terms with it. I knew that treatment for HIV had moved on so much that I could expect an almost normal life span – it wasn't an immediate death sentence, like it had been in the 1980s.

I decided to concentrate on the most important aspect of my life. What was it? I wondered. I concluded that my spiritual life was more important than the hedonistic side. I was ordained at the local temple of my Hare Krishna faith and focused on getting back to health. The medication I was on was working well for me, and within six months the virus was undetectable in my blood. My father and I had reconciled – perhaps the many years of physical and emotional distance between us had done us good. We had both moved on, and when I told him about my diagnosis, he was matter-of-fact about it but also supportive.

The relationship that didn't survive the diagnosis was the one I had with my long-term partner. After we split, I hit a downward spiral. I had coped well with my HIV diagnosis but now everything seemed very bleak. I'd come home from work, shut the door and wouldn't speak to anybody or do anything. At night I lay awake for hours, unable to sleep or relax. I left the temple and began attending my local Anglican church but I still felt very isolated.

I began seeing a psychiatrist regularly, and after some time had passed, she said, 'I want to run something past you, but it is a bit unusual.'

'OK,' I said.

'I've been using this quite successfully with other clients who are single, and that seems to be the key point. It works most effectively on single patients.'

I nodded, intrigued now by where this was heading.

'I thing you should try getting a pet, Barney, and more specifically, I think it should be a dog.'

'Really?' I hadn't expected that. 'What makes you think it will help my depression?'

'Well, a dog will be another living creature in the house when you get in and will be very happy to see you. It will need walks and exercise, and even if you're not in the mood, you'll have to do it for the dog's well-being. You'll start thinking outside yourself, and the more you go out with your dog, the more friends you'll make, and your social circle will increase.'

I'd been with my therapist for a long time and trusted her completely. What she'd said made a lot of sense. Ultimately, what did I have to lose?

'I've tried everything else from cognitive behavioural therapy to group therapy,' I told her. 'I'd like to give this a try.'

I began my preparations. For a while, I'd been volunteering at a homeless unit in London, a Monday-to-Friday commitment, working from nine till five every day. If I was to bring a dog home, I needed to make time for it, so I cut back my hours. Next, I had to decide if getting a puppy was the right thing for me. I didn't think I had it in me to go through all the house-training and, besides, I lived in a flat with no balcony or garden, which would make that all the more difficult. Also, I didn't want a puppy chewing things. I needed an adult dog.

One day, I was talking to a friend about it. 'Why don't you look at getting a rescue dog?' he suggested.

'Hmm,' I said. 'I hadn't really thought about that.'

He explained a bit more, and the more I heard, the more I liked the idea. 'I'm going to look into it because it's starting to sound perfect for me.'

I had a look online at Battersea Dogs & Cats Home. It was a charity that was close to my home and I was familiar with the name. Also, a few of my friends had taken in animals from there with much success and subsequent happiness. I spoke with a rehomer and found out I needed identification and a letter from my landlord to confirm that he was happy for me to have a dog in the flat. I didn't think he'd mind as his wife worked at a veterinary surgery and they were both dog mad.

I went along to Battersea, armed with my documents, and spoke to Sarah in the rehoming team. I had my full interview and told her about my flat on the Tower Hamlets side of Victoria Park. 'I'm two hundred yards away from the park,' I added. As we talked about what I was looking for, she agreed that a small or medium-sized adult dog would be the best fit for me.

We looked at a number of dogs but they all had multiple issues that made them unsuitable for me. Sarah was very understanding and wanted to make sure I was matched with the correct dog. 'This isn't something we should rush,' she said. I agreed. Although I had been ready to have a dog for six months, I wanted to wait for the right one. I continued viewing new dogs online but still none leapt out at me. I wanted a dog with a profile that spoke to me, and sometimes it was hard to keep motivated, especially in the winter when my seasonal depression reared its ugly head.

As we neared Easter and the days got longer and brighter, the depression began to ease and I realized I had to focus on finding a dog.

I arranged with two dog-owning friends to dog-sit for them for a week to see how I coped with it. The first was a Parson Jack Russell Terrier called Daisy. I stayed at her house for a week and took Daisy out for her usual three walks every day. Come rain or shine, Daisy's needs came first. I had wondered in the past if I would be able to put a dog's needs above mine if I was having a bad day but Daisy proved that I could. In the evening, she sat on the sofa and leant against me as I watched telly or worked on my laptop. She was wonderful company.

The following week, Buddy, a West Highland White Terrier, came to stay with me in the flat. He was a nutcase and a sweetheart all in one. I took him out three times a day and came to love how it felt to be out and about. I quickly got used to Buddy's energy, and having another being in the house. When I returned him to his owners and went home, it was as if a switch had been flipped inside me. Something was missing. The energy from another living creature was no longer in my flat and I knew then that a dog was the right choice for me.

I stepped down as a volunteer, leaving my job behind, and returned to Battersea. My original application had been suspended, as each is only kept live for six months. I chatted once more to a rehomer and told him, 'Everything in my life is completely the same, except now my employment is zero. I have one hundred per cent of my time to commit to a dog.'

A couple of weeks passed. On Sunday, as I got home from church, the landline began to ring. When I answered, it was Sarah from Battersea. 'Barney, I think I've found you the perfect dog. Leila has been fostered by one of our managers here and she's a good match for you. Would you like to meet her?'

I couldn't wait. 'Yes, please! When can I come in?'

Leila, a Jack Russell Terrier, was having her teeth done in the morning, so if I came on Tuesday afternoon, she would have recovered from the anaesthetic and be back to herself. 'Perfect,' I said.

I arrived on Tuesday at three o'clock with butterflies in my belly and a heart full of hope. Sarah greeted me and took me to a room where Leila was waiting with a handler. When I saw Leila, she instantly made me smile. She was running around the room, sniffing every nook and cranny, and when I sat down, she jumped up and put her paws on my knee. She wagged her tail and I bent closer to give her stroke. As I did so, she licked my nose and ran off again.

Sarah said, 'How did you do that?'

'Do what?' I asked.

Sarah said Leila was a sweet-natured dog but hadn't grown close to anyone, even her foster-mum, during her time at Battersea. Her licking of my nose was a sign of affection, which she had not displayed in her time at the kennels or during fostering.

As Leila continued wandering around, I learnt a bit more about her. She'd been in a house with the dog of her owner's sibling and the two hadn't got on. When push came to shove, it was Leila who'd got the boot. She was obsessed with her tennis ball, fussy with her food and had a tendency to pull on her lead. But all those things, with the right amount of dedication and time, could easily be worked out. I had a lot of time and could dedicate myself to Leila.

As my visit continued, I noticed that Leila had become a bit nervous as her initial excitement wore off. I guess, in a way, we were as nervous as each other. It was a big commitment, and now that I was so close to owning a dog, I wondered if I'd be able to cope with it. But the answer was to have a go. 'I'll take her, Sarah,' I said. After all, if I wanted my life to change, I had to make some changes. Leila was one of them.

Two hours later, we came out of Battersea, and Leila did indeed pull on the lead. Her whole body was telling me, *Faster, faster, let's go!*

We took the bus, and Leila hopped up on the front seat to stare out of the window. Considering she'd only met me a few hours earlier, anybody looking at us would have thought we'd been owner and dog for a long time. It seemed that out of the Home she was more herself.

When I got her back to my flat, we entered the lobby and she turned right on the landing before I took her that way. She went along the hallway and sat in front of my door. I reckoned she must have picked up on my scent as soon as we'd entered the building: she had homed in on my flat, no problem. I let her in and she ran around checking and smelling everything. When she was done, she jumped onto the sofa and settled down. Leila was home.

That night, she ignored her bed and followed me into my bedroom where she slept on the covers and hogged more than her fair share of the space available. If I tried to move her she snarled at me. I let her have that one. Next night, though, when she snarled as I tried to regain some space, I tipped her off. She soon learnt that if she wanted to enjoy the comforts of my bed, she had to share.

The first six months with Leila were a learning curve for both of us. I didn't know what had happened in her past, but Leila wasn't fully relaxed with me, and if I tried to pick her up, she'd growl. She was indeed fussy with her food, and I tried many different types until I found one she liked. At least that was one problem solved.

Next, I tackled the lead-pulling. There was a bit of a battle of wills between us to get the balance right, and I was frightened to let her off the lead in the park in case she didn't come back. But every day when we went for our walks, I started bumping into the same people also walking their dogs. They were a community and I became a part of it.

They all gave me advice on how to let Leila off the lead safely, but after two and a half months, one said, 'You're going to have to trust Leila at some point. Let her off when my dog's around too. They play together well and if Leila won't come back when you call her, I know mine will and she'll follow.' He was right and, to her credit, Leila coped fine with being off the lead and responded as she should when I called her back. After that I relaxed a bit, knowing I had lots of support from fellow dog-owners and Leila was being looked out for, not just by me but by all those around us. I just wished she would relax a bit too: she was still quite stressed out.

When fireworks season began, she was frightened and confused by the noise, and jammed herself as close to me as she could. It was nice that she was seeking comfort from me – things were definitely moving in the right direction. But it wasn't just Leila seeking comfort from me: I found myself seeking comfort from her too. If I was feeling particularly down or stressed, I'd spend time stroking and playing with Leila or taking her out for walks. My therapy sessions dropped from once a month to once every two months. My quality of life was improving with Leila around.

The winter came and went, and in February, it was as if a switch had been flipped in Leila's mind. She stopped battling me on everything and stopped snapping at me. It was as if she had finally given herself to me. She was no longer thinking she had to look after herself but realized that she could rely on me to look after her. She recognized that I was the one caring for her and that everything was OK now. She relaxed and became much more affectionate. If I had to leave her to go shopping or attend an appointment, when I got back I had to sit on the sofa for five minutes and let Leila lick my face. Before her light-bulb moment, she'd be happy to see me when I came home but not like this. Now I found Leila leading me to the bedroom so that we could cuddle on the bed or nap together. She had become the wonderful dog I had dreamt of and was making me very happy.

We fell into a natural rhythm and I found we could communicate though we couldn't speak the same language. If she walked away from me, I didn't force her to stay because I knew she would seek me out when she was ready. She knew I liked it when she sat next to me so she didn't go into her bed very often. I knew she liked to keep an eye on me most of the time and I wasn't obstructive: I left doors open so that if I was doing the dishes, or cleaning the bathroom, she could still see me. If I went out of view, she'd move so that she could see me.

As the trust and understanding between us developed, I began to get to know Leila's true personality. She was cheeky, knew her own mind, was very loving and affectionate to humans and other dogs alike. She liked big dogs in particular and was bold – she'd take a ball right out of another dog's mouth and wasn't afraid of anything.

Although Leila was a middle-aged lady of eight, she still had her mad moments, which brought a big smile to my face. One evening, we were outside talking to a neighbour with his dog when some fireworks were set off nearby. Leila and her doggy friend, Cyrus, bolted so we humans ran after them, thinking they'd been spooked by the noise. But when we caught up with them around the corner, I found Leila sitting and staring at the fish-and-chip shop. She loved their sausages so, as a treat, the dogs shared one.

She had some little quirks too. She wasn't a destructive dog so when I went out I didn't worry about my belongings, but Leila was obsessed with tennis balls. Whenever I went out, I often returned to find her tennis balls all over the house. It was like coming back to a ball pit instead of a flat! She didn't like getting her paws wet, and was happy most of the time, but she could be a bit of a madam. It didn't bother me, though, because I knew better than most that every human has bad days, so why should dogs be any different?

Time passed, and for the first time since my teens I felt content. My antidepressant medication remained at the same dose, but instead of having awful days when I no longer wanted to live, I started to think, *I can't do anything stupid because I have Leila to take care of*.

Before Leila, those days when I wanted to go to sleep and not wake up again happened every two or three months. With Leila in my life, it happens perhaps once a year. The seasonal depression still comes, and there's nothing I can do about that, but now I know it will go. I can shrug it off and look forward to the start of spring. I feel less stress and my friends have noticed I'm in a better mood and have more energy than before. The increase in energy is not only due to my emotional change: the walks I take daily with Leila have helped me lose four stone in weight and my waist has shrunk from forty-two inches to thirty-six. I'll be happy to lose another stone and another couple of inches, but that will be my lot.

Leila's body has changed too. She's solid muscle now, with all the exercise she gets and the good food she's eating, and though she's two kilos heavier than she was when I collected her from Battersea, she's leaner and stronger, too, with a defined arch under the leg and at her waist. Even my new dog-walking friends have noticed that, instead of scampering around, she has a healthy, effortless trot.

All in all, Leila and I have been very good for each other.

I'd lived on my own for a long time, and whenever I came home, it was silent and still. Everything was where I had left it, and the Internet was a blessing and a curse for someone like me with chronic depression. If I'd wanted to, I could have ordered everything I needed online and never left the house. For a person with depression, that is dangerous. But now, taking Leila out every day, I've broken the habit. I can't cut myself off, and when I do go out without Leila,

I look forward to coming home. In fact, if I'm out with friends and they suggest one more drink, I say, 'Sorry, but I have to get home to Leila.' She comes first and is my priority now. I get so much love from her – which makes me wonder why she was given up in the first place.

It wasn't until I was asked to take part in a film for the Who Needs Who campaign to promote rehoming at Battersea that the production team unearthed details about Leila's past. I learnt that she was born in April 2008 and microchipped that year. She spent six months with a family, then went to her next owner. Before her fifth birthday, she'd ended up on Gumtree. Her next owner went to prison, leaving Leila in his sister's care. She already had a dog, which was left alone in a room with Leila, unsupervised. The two had scrapped and then, of course, Leila was taken to Battersea, which was where I stepped in.

Now I understood why Leila had been the way she was when she first came to live with me. Perhaps she'd thought I would abandon her after a few months and it wasn't worth getting attached. But when she'd realized I wasn't going anywhere, she'd come out of her shell.

The film about Leila and me explored how she had changed my life and how I had changed hers and had 800,000 views online. It was a great success and I was happy to be part of such an important campaign.

To anyone reading this who is in my position, or who has experienced depression and mood problems, I would say, please consider getting a dog. Of course, it's best to find out if your therapist agrees that you're in the right state of mind for a pet, but if you are, then I urge you to consider a rescue dog. Getting Leila was the best thing I ever did and she is a part of me now. She has changed my life so very much for the better.

Surviving Amber

There was music coming from one of the rooms upstairs, and downstairs in the kitchen I could hear peals of laughter. The shared house I lived in with my boyfriend, Sam, was always packed with artists and musicians. It was wonderfully vibrant. But the most popular housemate was Amber, a German Shepherd Collie cross who had been rescued by Battersea Dogs & Cats Home and adopted by the homeowner before we'd moved in. Amber sauntered from room to room, playing with whoever would have her. We all looked after her and Pitou, a small Whippet cross and also a Battersea rescue dog.

It was great to have dogs in the house. In a way, Amber and Pitou gave the transient nature of our household a family atmosphere. The dogs were a constant presence, and while Pitou was much more inclined to snooze in a corner, Amber had the type of personality that everybody fell in love with – most of all me.

I'd grown up only ever having owned a guinea pig, but I'd dreamt of having a dog or cat. I had always loved animals, and whenever we'd holidayed in our summer home in France, the dog from the farm next door would meander on to our property to see us and snooze on our porch. He was very friendly and, in a lot of ways, much like Amber.

In our shared house, I was the only one who worked a nine-to-five job – with a wine company – so Amber had plenty of company during the day and volunteers to take her for a walk or a run around the park. Of course, she was quite large and needed a decent amount of exercise. She was also hugely sociable and curious by nature, and was happy to sleep in any of our housemates' bedrooms in that Victorian house in Lambeth. Somehow, though, over time, Amber began to show a preference. One evening, as she pushed open the door to our bedroom yet again and climbed onto our bed to have a cuddle with me, I felt a warm glow that she'd chosen me.

Time passed, and the homeowners made a decision. Sarah and Tom were moving to Berlin for work. The dogs, both rescues from Battersea, belonged to them and I felt a pang at having to say goodbye to Amber. As we discussed the options, though, we came to see that it might be best for Amber to stay with us. 'Amber is very attached to you,' Sarah said, 'and I don't think it would be fair to wrench her away.'

'I love Amber very much,' I said, 'and so does Sam. We're more than happy and willing to take full responsibility for her.'

There were other reasons for our developing arrangement. Pitou had become a bit jealous of Amber and rebelled every now and then. In fact, Amber had a new pink scar on her nose from a recent scrap they'd had. Sarah and Tom's new home in Berlin was a small flat and Amber would be too big to live there with them. It was decided that Amber would stay with Sam and me, while Pitou went to Berlin with Sarah and Tom.

Soon after, we said our goodbyes and it was very emotional for us all. Not only were Sarah and Tom heartbroken to say goodbye to Amber, but Sam and I were losing two close friends. I worried how Amber would react to the change in our household so I kept a close eye for any signs that she was pining for Sarah, Tom or even Pitou.

To my surprise, she didn't seem to notice that they had gone and just plodded on. Usually, there were people in and out of the house so she was rarely alone, but on the days when everyone would be out, I'd arrange to work from home so that Amber didn't get anxious. My working hours were flexible, and soon Amber and I fell into a new rhythm. I liked to run before work so Amber and I would go out together first thing in the morning, ending up at my parents' home, where she would stay for the day with them. After work, I'd pick her up and we'd stroll home together or run again. She was a healthy, active dog and loved the exercise we did together. We were an excellent match.

From time to time, ex-housemates would drop in just to visit Amber – that was how much she was loved by all who met her. When Sam moved to New York for a work opportunity, we did our best to keep our relationship going, as well as his with Amber. She pined for him so we Skyped in order that they could see each other but that didn't work very well: Amber wouldn't stay put and didn't seem to recognize his voice. In time, Sam and I decided our relationship had run its course and amicably ended it. We promised to stay friends, and whenever he came to London, he'd take Amber out and they'd have lots of fun together, roaming around Battersea Park, or going on road trips to the beach.

One week when Sam was back, I had a work conference and we arranged for Amber to stay with him for a couple of days. I packed her overnight bag, which went with her to my parents' home, usually with two days' worth of food, her favourite toys and her toothbrush. As I handed her over with her belongings, I couldn't help but laugh. 'It's like we're sharing custody of her.' He laughed too.

Next morning, I went to the conference and called Sam to check on Amber. 'Don't worry, she's fine,' he said. 'We've been doing lots of catching up.'

The following day, before I was due to pick her up, I missed a call from Sam. I was about to ring him back when a text popped up. As I read it, my palms turned sweaty. It was from Sam and it read: *Amber has had an accident. I'll call you back in a minute.*

I couldn't get my head around what Sam was saying. Had she slipped her lead and run into traffic? Had she somehow got out of the house? My head was in a spin as I tried to call him over and over again.

When he answered, I said, 'What's happened? Is Amber OK?'

As Sam explained, I began to cry. Amber had fallen out of a window: it was three floors to the pavement below. 'I'd taken her collar off for a wash earlier, so they didn't know who to contact. A passer-by called the police and Amber has been taken to Battersea for treatment. I'm trying to reach them now to see how she is.'

I hung up and ran outside to get on the first bus to Battersea. I was shaking and tearful and trying to hold it together until I reached my destination. But it was awfully hard. I replayed every word Sam had said over and over in my mind. I sat on the bus, willing it to get through the afternoon traffic.

Finally, at four o'clock, I arrived at the gates of Battersea and spoke to the security guard. He could see I was very shaken, and within minutes a vet from the clinic came out to talk to me.

'I think my dog has been brought here,' I said. 'She's been in an accident.' As I described Amber and all I knew about what had happened, Sam arrived. The vet explained Amber's current state: 'She's suffered serious injuries to her front paws and has major internal bleeding. We're trying to stabilize her so that we can move her to a specialist hospital for treatment.'

Sam's face was as white as a sheet, no doubt the same as mine. He told me that he had left Amber in the house while he was out during the day, and it was only when he returned that he discovered this awful thing had happened. I needed to focus on Amber so I asked Sam to leave. He did so, and the vet waved me through the security gates. As we walked quickly towards the clinic, she explained what she knew. Amber had fallen into the packed market below the window, where a woman at the scene who had worked for a vet comforted her until the police arrived.

The kind lady had kept the crowds back and also kept Amber still, then helped police officers get her into a squad car. She was brought straight to Battersea as she wasn't wearing a collar.

I was taken into a room next door to the surgery where Amber was. She was surrounded by the clinical team, who wanted to keep her calm. They'd given her pain relief and were trying to X-ray her to assess the damage she'd sustained in the fall. They were worried that if Amber saw me she might move or get agitated. She was in a great deal of distress and couldn't sit up, and the internal bleeding meant she couldn't breathe very well. I waited until she was quite sleepy with the medication before I went in to see her for a couple of minutes. Her paws were at odd angles and it was heart-breaking to see the state she was in. She was hooked up to drips and clearly out of it, but I knew she could hear me because when I stroked her head gently and said, 'I love you, girl,' she rolled her eyes to focus on my face.

I left the room in tears. It was a terribly distressing time and even the veterinary team were upset. The X-rays showed a massive internal bleed but it wasn't clear where exactly the blood was coming from. It was seven o'clock by now, way past the end of the team's shift, yet they all remained at work to try to stabilize Amber. I was so grateful to them for making such an effort for a dog they had never seen before and would probably never see again. They'd taken her in and cared for her when they didn't know anything about her – including, at that point, that she was a Battersea dog. I was in awe of the dedication they had shown.

The head vet called an animal ambulance to take Amber to a specialist hospital, but when it arrived, she changed her mind. 'I'm sorry,' she said, 'but Amber isn't stable enough. If we move her, it will kill her.'

The staff remained late into the night, as did the animal ambulance, and finally when Amber could be moved, she was taken to Elizabeth Street Veterinary Clinic, which deals with animal emergencies. I rode in the back of the ambulance, as did one of the Battersea vets, who continued to monitor Amber's vital signs and pain. He'd brought along a CD of all the scans and

X-rays taken at Battersea to hand over to her new medical team.

When Amber was unloaded, I hugged the Battersea vet. 'Thank you for all you did today. Your team were wonderful and I'll never be able to thank you enough.'

'We'll all be thinking of Amber and hoping she pulls through.' I tried to convince the vet to let me pay for the treatment Amber had received but he wouldn't hear of it.

Once inside, Amber was taken into a room for a full assessment and I called a friend to come and sit with me. The adrenalin from the shock was wearing off and I felt scared and alone, frightened of what might happen to Amber in the next few hours. My parents were on holiday in France and I didn't want to worry them until I knew more about Amber's condition. On the other hand, they loved her very much and I didn't want to keep it from them.

I called them and explained as much as I could about what had happened. They were as distraught as I was and Mum wanted to help. She called around and arranged for her best friend Martine's husband, Jeremy, to help move Amber if and when that was needed. Jeremy had taken many dogs from Battersea over the years and was keen to help out.

After some time, a vet came to see me and told me Amber's prognosis was not looking good. My chest tightened with anxiety. 'The damage to your dog's paws is extensive, and we don't know yet if it's fixable, but the bleeding she's having inside is the main concern.'

I learnt that when Amber had fallen out of the window, her elbows had jack-knifed into her chest, damaging her chest and lungs. If her diaphragm had ruptured, there was no coming back for her, especially at her age. Amber had been very fit and healthy but she was twelve.

Amber was given blood transfusions as well as a constant stream of painkillers and I was told the best place for her if she was going to survive was the Queen Mother Hospital for Animals in Hertfordshire.

'I don't want Amber to die,' I said, 'but I don't want to torture her either, treating her and moving her from one place to another. She's been through enough.'

We decided to see how Amber progressed overnight. I went home in despair and wrecked from the terrible events of the day.

Early the next morning, the vet called me to say Amber was stable enough to make the two-hour drive to the other hospital. I figured that as long as she was fighting to live, I'd do all I could to help her.

I took up Jeremy on his offer to help. He picked me up in his vintage Volkswagen camper van and took me to Amber. He'd cleared the back of the van and the vets helped him carry Amber out on a bed and place her in the back. She was whimpering with pain but very calm and still. She was more alert today and her eyes were glued to my face. I comforted her and talked to her, and an hour later, I looked up for the first time and saw that we were no longer in London. When we arrived at the Queen Mother Hospital, we learnt that the previous clinic had called ahead and referred Amber's case. They were expecting us and came outside with all the equipment needed to move her.

Meanwhile, Mum and Dad wanted to end their holiday early and come home to support me, but it was the anniversary of the D-Day landings and the ferries were packed. It should have taken longer for them to get home, but Mum was determined and they managed somehow to get onto a ferry. While they were travelling, I kept them in touch with updates.

The vet at the hospital assessed Amber once more and reiterated what I'd already learnt: Amber was in a very bad way. 'I don't want to keep her alive to live a life of pain,' I said. 'I don't want her to die but I have to be fair to her.'

He nodded. 'I understand but Amber is a very strong dog.'

'As long as she keeps going and fighting, I'm happy to support treatment, but I don't want to be cruel. I need you to advise me when enough is enough. I don't want to torture Amber just for my sake.'

We moved forward on that agreement and understanding. Stopping the internal bleeding was the priority and fixing Amber's paws had to take a back seat. Every day, my friends and I went to see my dog. She was up and down and I was desperate for my parents to get home. Finally, they arrived back from France, but by then, Amber had taken a turn for the worse. She had previously reacted to me and my voice, but now she was lying on her side, couldn't lift her head and was panting very hard.

We all listened as the vet explained Amber's most pressing problems were that her blood was failing to oxygenate and the internal bleeding. She was receiving extra oxygen and blood. 'We're giving her everything we can and at some point something has to start working. She can't survive indefinitely like this.'

'How much longer should we wait to see if she responds?' I asked.

The vet's face was grave as he said, 'We should give her another twenty-four hours of supportive care. Then we should make a serious decision. If her lungs continue to fail, her organs will shut down and we'll have to think about withdrawing life support.'

As we heard those words, we all went to pieces. We loved Amber so very much but I knew who each of us was thinking about as we faced the difficult day ahead. Six years earlier, my older brother, Dan, had become very ill. His blood was failing to oxygenate after he'd developed a rare side-effect to pneumonia. He had become critically ill and his lungs had stopped working, leading to his organs irreversibly shutting down. It had been extremely tough on all of us when, two weeks later, Dan died of acute respiratory distress syndrome – similar to what Amber was now facing.

The conversation we'd just had with the vet about Amber was strikingly similar to the one we'd had with Dan's medical team, and the cruel repetition of this scenario was just too much for us to bear. My parents and I went into a private side room, hugged each other and cried.

Later that evening, we left to go home, hoping beyond hope that Amber would pull through during the night and be on the mend by the morning. I was miserable, and my parents encouraged me to go to the pub with my friends for a couple of hours and try to clear my head. It was ten o'clock when I felt my phone vibrating in my pocket. *This is it*, I thought. *They're calling to tell me Amber's gone.*

But when I answered, I heard the best news. It was indeed one of Amber's vets. 'Emma, we wanted you to know that Amber's rallying. She's alert, sitting up, her oxygen levels have shot up and the internal bleeding has lessened.'

It was a huge relief. I phoned Mum and Dad straight away to tell them. The vet had told me they were giving Amber everything they could to help her get better and, just like he'd said, one of those things had finally helped turn things around. It wasn't possible to know which it was, but I wondered if all of us going to see her as a family had helped her rally in some way. It was a nice thought, if nothing else.

Next day, Amber was alert and reacting to us all. It was amazing to see how far she'd come in twenty-four hours. She hadn't been given any food since the accident, as it might have overloaded her system, but now it was time to feed her. The vets had asked us to bring along her favourite food so I had mackerel and cucumber with me. It might sound like a weird choice for a dog but, it really was her favourite. I gave it to her, unsure she'd have any appetite, but she gobbled it down.

Things continued like that for the next two weeks, and when she was better, I packed her favourite foods into a picnic basket, made some sandwiches for her human visitors, of whom there were many, and went to the hospital. The sun was shining so the nurses helped me wheel Amber on to a peaceful green next to the hospital. We sat in the sunshine and had a picnic. I'd never felt so grateful. Without all the wonderful people who had helped Amber, she wouldn't have been sitting there with me, munching her mackerel.

After that, Amber was strong enough to have surgery on her paws. The team explained that, ordinarily, they would operate on one paw at a time, but because of all the trauma Amber had endured, putting her under general anaesthetic twice was too risky. The vet said, 'I must warn you, this surgery is going to take your bill to eleven thousand pounds. Do you want to proceed?'

I didn't have that kind of money. 'I'll find it,' I said. My parents were in agreement. It was really important to the three of us that we did everything we could to fix Amber. After everything she'd been through, and the way we had lost Dan, it would have been cruel to lose Amber when we could do something to save her. It wasn't Amber's fault she'd had the accident, and dogs rely on us to keep them safe. The thought of her dying thinking we hadn't been there for her was not one I could live with. Whatever the cost, my family and I were saving Amber and piecing her back together. It was only fair after all the years of love and joy she had brought us.

I felt that even more keenly than my parents because when Dan had died Amber had brought me so much comfort. She hadn't been mine then, but she was such a happy young dog, who needed love and attention, and would happily spend hours with me, playing or sitting beside me, being my companion. In my darkest hours, Amber had kept me sane. Now it was my turn to support her.

The next day, two surgical teams were in the theatre with Amber, each working on one of her front paws. The joint in her paw that would be like a human's wrist or ankle was shattered on both sides. It wasn't something they could rebuild as the damage was severe, so both had to be replaced with metal plates and screws. The operation took four hours. Afterwards, Amber's paws were bandaged and she had a big plastic cone round her neck to stop her scratching at her many scars and stitches. I felt very sorry for her but Amber held up surprisingly well. It was as if she knew there was no other way through this but to tolerate everything and do as she was told.

Her survival was one thing and it was clear that she'd passed the most dangerous phase. But her recovery was going to be a long journey back to as good health as we could give her at her age. The vets strongly recommended hydrotherapy but Amber hated the water and I decided against it. I couldn't bear to put her through any more misery or discomfort than was absolutely necessary.

A week later, I took her home. I was instructed to keep her in one room for the next two months. The idea was to try to stop her doing anything that might cause her paws damage as they healed – for instance, jumping, climbing or ripping her stitches and getting an infection. She accepted her situation and was so good. Her patience and trust were amazing.

Wherever we went, people stared at us and I couldn't blame them. We were a sight to behold. Amber couldn't walk properly so she stomped her way along the pavement with plastic shopping bags wrapped around her front legs to keep the wounds from getting infected, and half her body had been shaved. People stopped me to find out what had happened and I'd recount the story as quickly as I could, my voice cracking while the person's eyes filled with tears. Amber's amazing strength and fighting spirit touched everyone who heard her story and she stood stoically beside me, her head up and her chest puffed out. She was such a beautiful and dignified dog, even in the state she was in, that I almost burst with pride.

Over the next few weeks, Amber developed an infection despite all the precautions we were taking, so the vet prescribed a course of strong antibiotics. She couldn't exercise or eat properly and lost weight, which was accelerated by the cocktail of anti-inflammatory pills she had to swallow. After a while, Amber decide the pain medications were making her stomach ache, and most probably making her feel sick, so I had to find increasingly creative ways to get them into her. I hid them in her favourite meats, in treats and even in dog sushi rolls. Most days, she would spit them out at my feet with a look on her face that told me, *You need to try harder than that.*

Eventually Amber yielded to the drugs, and got stronger. I returned to work after taking weeks off to care for her, and my parents and friends stepped in to dog-sit. Gradually, the difficult times began to fade and we began walking in the park. I noticed that when Amber broke into a run, she had developed a rocking-horse motion because of the pins and plates in her paws. But she didn't seem to care and neither did I.

Amber was there. She was alive and pain-free. That was more important than anything else.

I knew she really had her sparkle back when she started picking fights with any skateboards or bicycles she came across. Amber chased squirrels, barked at cats, stood staunchly in front of me when she didn't like the look of someone and still climbed up onto my bed for a snuggle every evening and morning. She behaved like a twelve-year-old puppy and it was so very endearing. It felt like the right time to send an update to some very special people.

One night, I opened up my emails and began to type:

Dearest Battersea Team, Some months ago, you helped my dog Amber when she had a terrible fall and arrived at your gates dying. I haven't been in touch until now because I wanted to write to you only when I had good news. Now, I have that good news and I am thrilled to share it with you. Amber has made an amazing recovery and she would really like to come and say hello to you all, and thank you for all you did to save her life. Without you, without your care, and without the dedication your team showed to her that fateful day, Amber wouldn't be here with me today.

Weeks later, Amber and I went to Battersea and this time there were only tears of happiness. She must have remembered the team because she was very excited to see them. I told them how grateful I was and that I would be indebted to them for ever for the critical care they had provided for Amber without so much as knowing her name. It was only then that the team found out that she had once been a Battersea dog. She'd been abandoned as a puppy beside a motorway and Battersea had stepped in to save her. It felt as though her life had come full circle. I hadn't been a part of Amber's adoption, but there we were, together, enjoying Battersea's legacy twelve years on.

After that visit, I vowed I would do whatever I could to help the charity, and that December, I took part in an Advent running fundraiser: instead of running a marathon in one go, I ran for a minimum of thirty minutes every day throughout the month, in Battersea's name, and raised £800. It wasn't much compared to everything the Home had done for Amber during her life, but I wanted to help in some small way.

I will always be so grateful for what Battersea did for Amber. Without them, Amber wouldn't be here today, and without Amber, I don't know where I would be.

Touched by Frost

It was the summer of 1999 and my boyfriend, Alex, and I were celebrating. We'd just bought our first home together in Middlesex and were settling in. We wanted to expand our household from two to three, but neither of us was quite ready for a baby. Then Alex had a thought. 'How do you feel about us getting a dog, Debbie?'

It was the perfect idea. Labradors were always a part of my family when I was growing up, and Alex wanted company when he was out working as a park ranger. We knew we could easily find a puppy, but as we had both the time and a happy home to offer a rescue dog the fresh start it deserved, we headed to Battersea Dogs & Cats Home. Its reputation for matching owners to dogs was unique and we were after a specific type of dog. There, I told a rehomer what we wanted. 'We're hoping for a female dog, suitable for training and able to go to work with Alex. He's a park ranger, out and about in his four-by-four all day.'

'It's good that you know what you want,' the rehomer said, 'because it makes it easier for us to suggest suitable matches. Why don't you have a look around the kennels while I go through our system?'

Alex and I took a walk around the kennels, and when I saw how many dogs were waiting for a new home, I was overwhelmed. It was heart-breaking to see the numbers that had ended up homeless through no fault of their own. I wanted to take them all home. But two hours passed and we hadn't seen any that really captured our hearts, so we returned to the rehomer, feeling a bit despondent. 'I've got one dog here,' she said. 'She's a Collie cross and about a year old. She's only been with us for a week so she's not quite ready for rehoming as we're still assessing her. But she could be what you're looking for.'

I was intrigued. 'Can we meet her?'

We were shown to a private room and Frost was brought in. She was white with a black patch over her left eye, a beautiful dog but clearly bewildered, a little hesitant and scared, if her tail was anything to go by. It hung limply between her back legs and she stood timidly away from us. But there was something about Frost that made my heart flutter. She looked at me and I knew for sure that the connection I had hoped to make with my dog was there. It was tentative, but it was there.

We learnt that a gentleman had found Frost wandering the streets without a collar and looking for food. He'd taken her in and kept her for a couple of weeks before bringing her to Battersea. Alex and

I played with her a little, as much as she would allow, and then we were left to have a chat about what to do. 'I want her, Alex. Do you?' He nodded.

The rehomer agreed that we were a good match. 'We'll need a letter from your employer, Alex, to confirm that Frost can come to work with you. Is that all right with you?'

'No problem.'

We went home and got ourselves ready for Frost's arrival. I told our neighbours we were bringing a dog home and there might be some excited barking until we got her settled in. They were fine about it so I went shopping for a dog bed, harness, lead, toys and food. Alex got the letter from his boss, and the following weekend we drove to Battersea, ready to pick up Frost.

We waited in the Lost and Found reception area, and I wondered if Frost would recognize us. When she came through the door, she spotted us and her tail started wagging. It was clear she did remember us and she looked brighter that she had last time. We decided to keep her name as we loved the one Battersea had given her.

As we had a bit of a car journey back to our house, we decided to take her for a walk in Battersea Park first. She was so striking-looking that she attracted a lot of attention and people stopped to talk to us. I felt proud of her already and told everyone who asked that her name was Frost and she was a Battersea dog.

Soon, we began the ninety-minute drive home, and I sat in the back with Frost to keep her calm. When we arrived I let her into the house and her tail shot up. She trotted around, taking it all in.

Within days, we felt as though Frost had always been with us. She lounged on the sofa when she thought nobody was looking, had a favourite toy stashed in every corner and knew exactly when her dinner was due. She'd come and stare at us if we were a minute late with it. We quickly learnt she was very good at being obedient and took to training well. But she was a young dog and had her mad moments. She couldn't help being a bit noisy in the group lessons when the excitement got to her. I also hired a private trainer, who would come to our home and work with Frost in the garden.

The main issue we had was that Frost would jump up at people when they came into the house and we hadn't been able to combat it alone. The trainer advised us to turn our backs on her and ignore her until she learnt that she wouldn't get our attention by bouncing up at us. It was such simple advice, and when we asked all our guests to implement it, Frost soon stopped jumping up at them.

By now, Alex was taking her to work with him every day and she was loving being outside so much. When he was driving the four by four, he used the red harness I'd bought to clip her to the seatbelt and she loved riding around with him. It was great for Alex, too, as his job could be quite solitary at times, driving through the acres of land, tending it, clearing debris and doing whatever else had to be done. For the first time in years, he had a lovely companion by his side all day long. Frost thoroughly enjoyed being with him in the four by four, and when he was in the office, she'd curl up under his desk in a little bed we'd bought for her.

At the weekends, we took Frost to the park around the corner from our house and worked with her on her recall. Before long, we had her running between us and responding to her name. Even if one of us hid out of view and called her, Frost came running. She was everything we had hoped for, and enriched our lives so much.

The following year Alex proposed and I happily accepted. When we planned our wedding we decided we wanted Frost to be part of it. On the big day, she came with us to the church, and I had a figurine made of her for our wedding cake. Our guests loved that and thought it was very sweet that we'd involved her to that extent. For us, however, it had been a no-brainer. Frost wasn't just our dog, she was an integral part of our little family and featured in most of the wedding pictures.

The week after the wedding, Frost stayed with my mum while we jetted off to Lake Garda, Italy, for our honeymoon. It was wonderful and romantic but I did miss our Frostie girl, as I called her. She was very happy to see us when we returned, although it was clear she'd had lots and lots of fun staying at Grandma's: every time we neared Mum's house in the car from then on, Frost began barking and whining in anticipation of seeing her special friend.

Life went on and, of course, Alex still loved taking Frost to work with him. She adored sticks, and whenever they were near the park's wood pile, she would find the biggest stick she could get her teeth around. Alex was in tears of laughter as he told me, 'I wish you could see her. She picks sticks so big that her back legs shoot up in the air when she tries to carry them.' I could imagine the scene because I'd seen her do the same thing during our weekend woodland walks.

Our girl had so much personality and I enjoyed getting to know her quirks. Frost loved having her tummy tickled, squeaky toys, sitting on our laps and running all over the house when she was feeling hyper. She loved being on the beach near Mum's house in Hampshire and wasn't scared of big waves. The three of us spent a lot of time together there and Frost loved jumping around and swimming in the sea.

When Frost was four, we decided to move to Weymouth. We liked being on the beach so much that we wanted it to be permanent. Alex found a job quickly and went to work with kids in an activity centre. For the next three months I was at home with Frost. It was lovely to have such quality time with her but Alex missed her terribly. After a few months, I accepted a job in a college to begin a couple of months later.

Before my start date, I began thinking about what we'd do with Frost during the day while I was at work. Then one morning, the letterbox flapped and a card fell through from Karen, who lived nearby and was starting out in dog walking. I gave her a call and we met up, along with Frost. She took a shine to Karen so I decided to go ahead with her.

Every day, Karen took Frost out while Alex and I were at work. Karen was new to dog walking and Frost was her first client. I felt proud: Karen found that our dog's special personality gave her confidence to continue building her business.

Karen called her Princess Frostie because of her attitude to the other dogs. 'Frost thinks she is the queen bee,' she told us, 'and she puts the new dogs in their place. Now they all follow her lead!' It was so reassuring to know that she was in such good hands when we were out working.

One day we had some news. I was pregnant. We were very excited to be having a baby but I did worry a little about how Frost would cope when she was no longer the centre of attention, especially given that she liked to boss the other dogs in Karen's walking group around.

When our daughter Amy was born, I realized my fears were completely unfounded. Frost was very calm and only a little curious about the mewing bundle that now ruled our house. She wasn't jealous and didn't interact with Amy very much until she started toddling. Then, as Amy grew into a lively little girl, Frost kept a protective eye on her. She followed Amy around, and even when she was napping, Frost lay at her feet.

While everyone else in our household was fine, I started to feel a bit depressed. When Amy was nearly four, I realized I had never dealt with the post-natal depression I'd come down with after giving birth, and the effects still lingered. Also, I wasn't happy with my job and I missed being near Mum. Frost was very comforting. Sometimes I'd feel teary and she'd plant herself next to me, not moving till I'd cheered up. She was a compassionate dog and I loved having her around when I was feeling sad. A dog doesn't ask why you're crying, and you don't have to talk when you don't feel like it, but it will still be there for hugs and comfort.

Eventually, Alex and I decided to move closer to Mum in Hampshire, before Amy started school: we didn't want to uproot her after she'd settled in. Once we were in our new home, I took a part-time job in the local library. Amy started school, and six months later, I was able to stop taking the antidepressants I'd been prescribed. Things were on the up again.

When I was at work, Frost went to Mum's house and loved being there. They had a very special relationship and whenever I went to pick her up, Frost hovered in the doorway, reluctant to leave. Deep down, I knew she would have been quite happy to stay with

Mum permanently because she was so attached to her. But the thought of Frost not being around was unbearable. She had been with Alex and me from the moment our life as a couple had begun in earnest. She'd been there as we settled into our first home, got engaged, married and then had a baby. She had moved house with us twice and shared every holiday, except our honeymoon, that we had ever taken.

Luckily for us, Frost was a fit and healthy dog and wasn't showing any signs of slowing down. The only problem she'd had the whole time she'd been with us was a bout of vestibular neuritis in her inner ear, which had affected her balance until medication cured it.

As Amy grew older, her relationship with Frost began to develop properly. Just as Frost had been at Alex's side at work, then at mine through my depression, now she was Amy's right-hand dog. When Amy rode her bicycle, Frost trotted alongside her, keeping a watchful eye on her. When we were out and about, if anybody came too close to Amy, Frost positioned herself between Amy and the stranger. They, too, had developed a special bond over the years. Wherever we went, Frost courted attention, just like she had all those years earlier in Battersea Park. Nobody could believe she was sixteen.

Christmas that year came and went, and in January I posted a picture of Frost on my Facebook page, with the caption: *Our Frostie girl is now entering her seventeenth year. What a lucky family we've been to know her.* Dozens of people commented that she didn't look her age.

Soon after, I took Frost for a walk to the football pitch near our home and noticed she was a little wobbly on her back legs. I wondered if she'd picked up a bug and wasn't feeling great. But when Alex, Amy and I took her for her second walk later that evening, we saw she was having difficulty moving and going to the toilet.

She began to deteriorate so we took her to the vet and learnt that her age had finally caught up with her. We didn't want to put her through weeks of investigation and medication, and if it was Frost's time, we'd do what was right for her. The vet agreed we could wait until my mum had returned from her holiday in Mexico in two weeks' time. I didn't want to tell her what was going on with Frost over the telephone and I didn't want to take any drastic action before she had returned and could say goodbye properly.

For the time being, Frost was eating well and didn't appear to be in any pain but her back legs were losing strength with each passing day. She was so strong that when she was having an episode, she would move around the house by dragging herself with her front paws. But it was clear that she didn't have long to go. Alex made her a sling and we would take her outside using it to hold her back half up so that she could propel herself forward without putting any weight on her hind legs.

I willed Mum to come home so that we could do what was best for Frost. At work, I struggled to cope with what I knew was coming and rushed to the loo in floods of tears whenever I thought of saying goodbye to my dog. It was awful knowing that Frost would soon be leaving us. She had been part of our family for so very long and the thought of her not being with us any more made me feel lost.

I made sure to take lots of pictures of Amy with Frost and snapped them lying on the floor together, or snuggling on the sofa. Those were the moments I wanted never to forget. We put paint on Frost's paws and pressed them against a canvas, made a plaster cast of one paw and took clippings of her coat to keep.

When Mum returned, she called to tell me all about her holiday but within a couple of minutes, she said, 'Darling, what's the matter? Has something happened?'

'Mum,' I said, my voice cracking, 'it's Frost. She's not well.'

We spoke for a long time, through tears, and decided Friday would be the day we'd all take Frost to the vet. I made the appointment, then arranged for Frost to be cremated individually and her ashes returned to us. On the dreaded day, we all drove to the vet's surgery. Mum and Amy said their goodbyes and left the room while we stayed with Frost as the vet administered the drug. Alex and I stroked her and talked to her, whispering how much we loved her and would miss her. I'm sure she understood because she wouldn't take her eyes off us. I was heartbroken as I watched her close them for the last time. Alex and I clung to each other as Frost took her last breath.

Eventually we emerged to comfort Mum and Amy. We all hugged each other for a long time. It had been such an awful day but none of us wanted to return to a house without Frost so we went to the local pub instead. We forced down a meal, then raised a glass to our Frost.

'I feel like I'm right-handed and now I'm trying to use my left hand,' Amy said. It was her eight-year-old way of expressing how wrong things felt without our dog. I couldn't have put it better myself.

Alex collected Frost's ashes from the vet and we placed her urn on the mantelpiece, along with the Battersea collar she'd worn and the canvas of her paw prints we'd taken only weeks earlier.

Amy was very upset but children are resilient and she coped well with her sadness. I, though, was grief-stricken. I worked three days a week and up to now the other four days had been filled with walks and Frost. Now they were empty. I began to feel depressed. I realized I had known Frost for seventeen years and my grandmother for just fourteen before she had passed away. Frost had been a huge part of our family's life and the grief I felt at losing her was as intense as if she had been human.

I knew that Alex was having a hard time, too, so I didn't want to go on and on about it. I didn't want my sadness to exacerbate my family's pain. I didn't feel able to tell my work colleagues or friends how down I felt about my dog in case they thought I was being ridiculous, getting things out of proportion. Instead I turned to the Internet where I found an online chat forum for bereaved pet owners. Hundreds of people were describing exactly how I felt. I registered my details and started a profile, enabling me to communicate with the other members.

I spent hours looking through and reading stories, viewing pictures and chatting to others in my situation. It was such a comfort to talk about Frost in that safe space and share stories about her without upsetting the people I was talking to. I told them about the time she'd disappeared from the garden at Mum's house, only to return with fishing line hanging out of her mouth. She'd swallowed a fish hook whole and had needed surgery to retrieve it! And once, when I had been too scared to get in the sea near Mum's, Frost had raced ahead and paddled out till she was just a dot, forcing Alex and me to go in after her. I told them about how my life felt empty without her and how much I missed her. The forum folk were very supportive, and as we chatted, I came to understand my grief better. I wasn't just missing our special Frost but the companionship of a dog. I missed going outside every day and walking in the fresh air, come rain or shine.

I signed up to a website that connects dog owners with other locals who want to spend time with dogs. In my days off work, I began walking an elderly lady's dog, but it wasn't the same as coming home to a dog of my own. I missed getting licked to death if I made the mistake of lying on the sofa or having a dog under my feet as I tried to cook. I missed the little things that made having a dog so much fun.

For five months, life felt a bit strange and empty. Then Alex and I began talking about getting another dog. Neither of us would ever want to replace Frost but we needed that presence in our home. We decided to start looking for another Collie after our summer camping holiday in Dorset.

We stayed on a farm for our holiday and spent the days walking and our nights cooking by the campfire as a family. It was quite cathartic and perhaps what we all needed. There were working farm dogs around us, and when I heard that one had given birth to a litter of puppies, I had to see them for myself. I went to the house and asked the owner if I could meet them. 'Of course you can,' she said. 'Follow me.'

She showed me to an enclosure in a sheltered barn where a gorgeous litter of ten-week old Border Collies wriggled this way and that, yelping happily. Each was as beautiful as the next. But one little black-and-caramel puppy was very chilled out and sat on a bale of hay above the others. She was watching the world around her with curious eyes. I returned on the next four evenings and couldn't keep my eyes off that puppy.

On the final day of our holiday, I took Alex with me. 'I think she's the one for us.'

'She's gorgeous.'

I spoke to the owner and we were able to take the puppy out of the enclosure and play with her for a while. She was so sweet, gentle and calm. Amy was very taken with her and begged to take her home with us.

I spoke once more with the owner, who was happy for us to take her home but said we'd have to wait another week till she was twelve weeks old. It was a ninety-minute drive to the farm but that didn't matter. 'Fine by me,' I said. 'Will you please promise to keep her for us?'

'Of course I will. She's your puppy; I just want to make sure she leaves her mum at a time when she's ready.' I was glad she was so responsible.

We returned home and prepared our house for the puppy's arrival. The stair gates went up and we secured the garden to make sure she couldn't escape out of any gaps in the fence and hedges. We hadn't needed any of that for Frost as she'd been older so this was new to us.

As we got things ready for Tilly's arrival, I started to feel an odd sense of guilt. I didn't want to feel we were moving on from Frost because none of us would ever forget her and how special she was. My guilt at bringing a new dog into our home didn't let me feel much excitement.

A week later, Alex and I returned to the farm to pick Tilly up. The lady gave us a bag of food, and I asked if we could take some of the hay Tilly had been sleeping on. I hoped the familiar smells would ease her transition from farm to house puppy. That turned out to be entirely unnecessary: Tilly was sturdy, strong and didn't suffer any separation anxiety. She slept on the sofa bed in the dining room and ignored the hay bed I'd made for her. When I took her to the vet to be checked over, he said she was from strong working stock and a very healthy puppy.

In the months ahead our house was chaotic. Tilly was mad about balls and loved to play. She was a finder, too, and brought us anything she'd found in the garden or in another room in the house. She was very obedient, but if we didn't pay her enough attention, she brought in one of Amy's wellingtons or my slippers and began to chew them in front of us. That made us sit up and react!

She was very smart and knew just how to push our buttons, and sometimes she'd look at us in a way that reminded me so much of Frost. It was painful at times but also comforting to see Frost's Collie traits coming through in the new addition to the family.

I knew we'd made the right decision, though. We've all been so much happier since Tilly arrived, and Amy especially enjoys having a puppy to play with. Tilly is excitable and wants to play no matter what time of the day or night it is.

Once more, Mum is dog-sitting while I am at work and already I can see a special bond forming between her and Tilly.

Tilly has helped ease our pain at losing Frost. She has become our focus, another dog that needs love and friendship. If she can be half the dog Frost was, I will be very happy for many years to come. However much time and effort you put into a dog, you'll get the same, and then much more, back. It's our joy to start this new journey with Tilly and I look forward to what the future holds for our family.

Our Black Pearl

It had been a trying time for my husband, John, and me. We'd entered retirement expecting life to run smoothly, for things to be more relaxed. But somehow everything had become tougher. John had hurt his ankle and his recovery had been very long and slow. He'd lost a fair degree of his mobility and it was taking its toll on us both. Meanwhile, our daughter Judy was having mental-health problems and she'd moved back in with us to try to recover. Together, we were muddling along, hoping for brighter and better days for our family.

One morning over breakfast, I voiced an idea that had been rattling around in my mind for a while. 'How would the two of you feel about getting a dog?'

John and Judy looked at each other and then back to me. 'I think that's a lovely idea, Maggie,' John said.

Our family needed a new and happier focus, and a dog would provide one.

John began researching online and found we could make an email application to rehome a dog from Battersea Dogs & Cats Home. We filled out the form: John and I were retired, were available all day to take care of a dog, and had a big, secure garden. Within days, I was called by a rehomer at Battersea Old Windsor and we were invited to come in and view the dogs available.

The three of us set off in the car, and when we arrived, we were shown to the kennels by a lady called Alison. She gave us some time to look around and told us to come and find her in the office when we were done. We thanked her and set off around the kennels. I was sad to see so many Staffordshire Bull Terriers waiting for new homes. My stepfather had always had Staffies and I had grown up with a soft spot for them, knowing how loving and loyal they could be.

As we walked through, Judy stopped at a kennel and read out the name of the dog inside. 'Maisy. She looks sweet, doesn't she?'

I glanced in and saw a brindle-and-black Staffie trotting towards us with her tail wagging and a twinkle in her eyes. She looked at each of our faces in turn and, though she didn't bark, her soft gaze was telling us, *Hello, it's nice to see you!* She seemed very friendly so we asked Alison if we could meet her. We were taken to a private room and Alison came in with Maisy. 'Whose dog will she be?' she asked.

'Mine,' I said, stepping forward. Given Judy's health, and John's ankle, I would be responsible for all walks and care. Alison gave me some treats to help me get to know Maisy a little. I threw her a ball and she fetched it for me, stopping with me for a stroke. She was very affectionate and cheerful and I thought she was wonderful. 'What do you know about her?' I asked.

We learnt that Maisy was between one and two years old and had come into Battersea having already had a litter of puppies, perhaps even two. It appeared she had been used as a breeding bitch, before she had been found by a member of the public, wandering the streets looking lost and frightened. She was still only eleven kilos after a month of Battersea's specialist care. This was underweight – she should have weighed fourteen or fifteen. Whoever had kept her before she was rescued had not taken good care of her. If anything, her owner had been negligent.

Maisy circled around us, tail wagging, as we discussed her past, present and future. While the details on her past were sketchy, her future, at least in my eyes, was crystal clear. Maisy was coming home with us. 'We'd love to take her, please,' I told Alison.

'I think you'll be a great match. Maisy is very intelligent and loves company so she's a good fit for your family – you have plenty of time to dedicate to her.' We would have loved to take her home there and then but Battersea had to run a car tolerance test on her to make sure she could handle the ninety-minute drive to our home.

A few days later, I received a call from Alison. 'We took Maisy out in one of our vans and you'll be pleased to hear that she hopped up on the seat and promptly fell asleep for the duration of our journey. She'll be absolutely fine on the drive back to your house.'

'That's wonderful news. Thank you for doing that. When can we collect her?'

Maisy had kennel cough so we waited a few weeks until it had cleared up. Then I returned with Judy to pick her up. She was lovely, and so happy to see us. She was an angel in the car on the way home, which gave Judy and me time to talk about Maisy's name. Many new owners change their rescue dog's name but I'd looked up what 'Maisy' meant on the Internet. It was thought to have come from the Latin name 'Margarita', meaning 'pearl'. I had once read a romantic legend about where pearls came from: apparently, the ancient Persians believed that when oysters broke the surface of the sea to gaze at the moon, a single drop of dew formed in their shells, which, when touched by the moon's beam, turned to pearl.

'Oh, Mum, that's beautiful,' Judy said, when I told her the story. 'We shouldn't change Maisy's name.'

The way that Maisy had gazed at us in the kennel that day, and her lovely temperament, made her a very rare black pearl to us. Her name would stay, as would she.

When we arrived home, I decided to take her to one of the fields in our little village for a walk to shake off the long car journey. As I leant down to put her lead on, its other end swung towards her and she cowered away from me. I was horrified. Just what had she been through? Had she been hit by her previous owners, as well as starved and treated as a puppy-making machine?

I stroked her gently and eventually I was able to click on her lead. We headed outside, cleared the road and went into the field. It was as if Maisy had never been for a walk or seen rolling countryside. She was very excited and that afternoon we both enjoyed being out together.

That night, she fell asleep quite early on and didn't cry or bark. I found myself waking up every now and then, worried that Maisy might feel frightened in her unfamiliar surroundings, but she slept soundly and peacefully.

The next morning, John and I came down to find Maisy not on her bed where we'd left her, but on the cold kitchen floor. I moved towards her and ran my hands over her head and down her back. She let out a low growl. I pulled my hand back and the noise in her throat continued. 'I think she's growling at me, John.'

He shook his head. 'That's not growling. Maisy's wheezing.'

I listened again and realized he was right. I looked over the list given to us by Battersea, telling us about the common signs of rehoming stress to look out for, such as separation anxiety, toileting in the house, general anxiety as to where to sleep and about new routines, to name but a few, and this wasn't one of them. She was clearly ill so I took her to a nearby vet immediately. It was lucky I did: Maisy had developed a rare side-effect of kennel cough – canine pneumonia. She was very poorly indeed and was started on a course of strong high-dose antibiotics.

She stayed at the surgery overnight and I barely slept a wink, but next morning, the vet called to say Maisy was showing some improvement. We could bring her home but we were warned not to throw a ball in case Maisy ran after it. A racing heart so soon after pneumonia could trigger a heart attack in a dog as underweight as Maisy.

In time, Maisy made a full recovery. She no longer wheezed and her weight gradually increased to fifteen kilos.

Next, it was John's turn for a hospital stay. He needed an operation on his ankle. The first night he was away, I returned home and was fixing a snack in the kitchen when a blur of orange movement beside me made me scream. It was a little fox cub that had come into the house through the open patio door. By the time Maisy had run in to see what the fuss was about, the cub had disappeared. I fetched my neighbour, Jeff, to look for it but he couldn't find it. I reckoned it must have scooted out of the patio and back to where it belonged while I'd been at Jeff's house.

The next day, I picked up John from the hospital and brought him home. He was hobbling about on a

zimmer frame and I hoped Maisy's energetic movements wouldn't cause him any trouble. But, to my
amazement, it was as if she understood that he needed
extra time to move about and was even slower on his
feet than usual. She kept him company on the sofa as
he recovered.

While he was recuperating, John avoided the stairs
and slept on the sofa downstairs. One night, he heard
Maisy barking so he shuffled into our piano room
where she had taken to sleeping. 'Come on, then, let's
go outside for a wee,' he said. But Maisy wouldn't
budge.

Three days passed and we were watching the wedding of Kate Middleton and Prince William when
Maisy started sniffing around the piano and trying to
get our attention from the other room. 'Can you move
that piano, darling?' John asked.

'No, John, it's very heavy!'

'I know, but something near it is bothering Maisy.
Will you check it?'

I got up and did as John requested. As I turned the
piano around, two pointy orange ears, a bushy tail and
two terrified eyes peered up at me from the back of the
instrument. I gasped. It was the little fox cub I'd lost
track of days earlier! 'Oh, my goodness!' I said, and
rushed out to fetch a broom. With it, I gently ushered
the cub towards the patio doors while Maisy watched,
calm as could be. She wasn't alarmed in the slightest.
When the drama was over, she followed me into the

lounge and stared at us both, clearly very pleased with herself.

'That must have been why she barked in the middle of the night,' John said. It made perfect sense now. But what didn't make sense was why Maisy hadn't done anything to alert us to the cub's presence. Instead, she'd spent a few nights sleeping in the piano room with it! It showed how tolerant a dog Maisy was to put up with the intruder in our house instead of flushing it out. The cub had been very young and was probably bewildered. Maybe Maisy had felt a maternal need to comfort it, or perhaps she'd stayed in the room to keep an eye on it as John and I slept.

As John's recovery continued, I took Maisy on daily walks near our village. Her favourite was in the fields across the road from our home. On the way, we passed the local horticulture centre. As a retired teacher of special-needs children, I knew the centre provided sheltered employment for adults with learning difficulties, and sometimes we'd bump into the team as they tended the centre's gardens with wheelbarrows full of plants. Maisy always had her ball in her mouth and the adults there loved seeing her. She'd stop by someone's feet and drop her ball, waiting for her chosen human to throw it for her. I had learnt it was her way of making friends and she often made very good choices. The person she'd drop the ball for was almost always partial to a game of catch. One of the young men there was her all-time favourite and was always impressed by how well she could catch. Maisy loved to run as fast as she could, then use her back legs to propel herself into the air and grab the ball in her teeth. 'She'd make an excellent goalkeeper for England,' one chap said.

I signed Maisy up for obedience classes with the Kennel Club and we started with basic dog training for a bronze award. As she wasn't a pedigree, she couldn't automatically get a pet passport to travel to France with us, where we liked to visit friends, but I'd heard that Kennel Club award certificates might qualify her. She had come to us knowing how to sit, which she'd learnt with Battersea, and she was so intelligent that it seemed a waste not to try for the Kennel Club awards. She turned out to be just as good as I'd hoped at picking up new moves and tricks, and before long, she could stay, come and heel. Because her interest in balls was so high, the trainer reckoned Maisy would make an excellent working dog at a place like Luton Airport. She flew through her bronze and silver awards, and then it was time for the gold.

It was quite tricky and I hoped Maisy would pull off all the elements. First I told her, 'Stay down,' and had to walk away from her, leave the room, return and tell Maisy to stay down while I circled around her. For the next test I had to walk with her off the lead and to heel, without her being distracted by other dogs in the room. The final step was telling Maisy to sit, moving away some distance, then telling her to come towards me. She had to be able to stop and start that walk to me on command.

We passed, and I was so proud of her.

When we had finished all the classes, I applied for a pet passport again, but the rules relating to dogs travelling to France had changed, and Maisy was still excluded. 'I needn't have bothered putting in all those hours,' I grumbled to John.

'But Maisy loved it, didn't she?'

That was true. I knew Maisy had the potential to do something special but I wasn't sure what it would be. I just knew that she had something soothing about her, and anyone who came into contact with her felt it.

It was to come in handy one Christmas when my niece visited us with her two young daughters. Sian, who was eight at the time, had developed an extreme fear of dogs ever since an Alsatian had knocked her over as a tiny child. She refused to be in the same room as Maisy and I did my best to keep my dog away from her: the last thing I wanted was for Maisy to exacerbate Sian's fear. One afternoon, we all went for a walk and Maisy took a shine to Sian's older sister, Katherine. Katherine was enchanted with Maisy and played with her around the park, chasing her and throwing a ball again and again. She was delighted every time Maisy returned the ball to her feet. Sian watched with trepidation but I could tell her brain was ticking over.

After Christmas I wrote a story about Maisy's life and personality, and all the things she liked doing, and posted it to Sian. I hoped it would help her understand that good dogs were nothing to be frightened off. She wrote back and gave me five stars for the story. I was happy with that and hoped that the next time we saw Sian she would be more comfortable around our dog.

Sure enough, next time we saw Sian, she was a bit calmer. She wouldn't touch Maisy but she seemed less nervous and would stay in the room if Maisy was there. After that, every time we were together, I noticed further improvement in Sian, which made me very happy. There was just something very calming about Maisy.

Some time later my neighbour Astrid gave me some sad news. Her son Roger and his wife, Stephanie, had a little boy called Tom. While Stephanie had been expecting their second baby, she had suffered a sudden cardiac arrest and died. Roger had not only lost his young wife but his unborn baby too. His life had been ripped apart. It was a terrible time for the family and Tom was spending a lot of time with his grandparents as Roger tried to come to terms with his loss.

I hoped I might be able to cheer Tom up a little. My granddaughter Isobel loved nothing more than being lifted in our arms to pick apples from our tree when she was visiting with her parents from America. 'Would you like to bring Tom over to pick some apples in our garden?' I asked Astrid.

She agreed, and Tom enjoyed picking apples, but more than that, he was fascinated with Maisy and returned to play with her whenever he was with Astrid. Sometimes Roger came too and we all took Maisy for walks. Tom was tiny but he liked to think he was holding Maisy's lead when we walked her around the green near our house. In fact, I was holding the lead above his head where he couldn't see it. Maisy was wonderful. When Tom threw the ball for her, she returned to him slowly, dropped the ball and stepped back so that he wasn't intimidated by her. She made it clear that she'd wait for Tom to pick it up in his own time and throw it for her.

She never extended the same courtesy to me: she usually became so excited she'd reach towards me every time I picked the ball up, or if I didn't pick it up quickly enough she'd position the ball so I'd trip over it. But with Tom, just as she had been with Sian and the young man with special needs, Maisy was careful and measured in her movements.

When Tom was six, we did a sponsored walk for the charity Cardiac Risk in the Young to raise money for research into the cause of cases like his mother's. The whole village was supportive, and Maisy came with us wearing a red jacket with CRY on the back, handmade by my friend Margaret, who lived in the village, to let everyone know which charity we were walking for. We raised £1,400 for Cardiac Risk in the Young by walking forty-eight miles over eight days. By then Maisy was seven and had developed a touch of arthritis in her hip but she could still walk around six miles a day comfortably, as advised by the vet.

Tom and Roger joined us to walk whenever they could, and at the end, we were greeted in the village by a welcome committee of all those who had joined us on various days of the walk. There was a raffle, tombola and a picnic on the green. It was wonderful to feel the community spirit and to see everyone who had supported us. But I wouldn't have been surprised if everybody had just come to see Maisy. She had a huge fan-club and made friends wherever she went. I reckoned Maisy was the most popular girl in the village.

The following summer, Tom was still popping over to see Maisy. I had an idea, which I put to his dad. He liked it, so I emailed Tom: 'Would you like to enter a competition for best young dog handler with me?'

Moments later, he replied: 'Yes, I'd love to.'

We wouldn't have as much time to train as some of the others because Maisy wasn't Tom's dog so they weren't together all the time, but I hoped that, if nothing else, it would give Tom something to look forward to.

On the day, Roger came with Tom.

'Tom,' I said, 'there are some children entering who are twice your age and have spent much more time with their dog.'

He understood what I meant: that he might not win or do well. However, he was thrilled to be taking part. 'I won't get upset, Maggie, I promise.' I spent ten minutes talking through what would be expected of him and Maisy in terms of obedience tests, and also about the short agility course.

Tom's name was announced over the speaker and they set off together. Roger, John and I watched proudly as Tom and Maisy flew through the tests. When our pair was placed fourth, we all whooped and cheered with delight. I was so impressed: their result showed how much trust and friendship Tom and Maisy shared. It was a very proud moment.

As Maisy's arthritis progressed I realized that the agility classes were no longer viable for her as she couldn't make the jumps any more. I did a bit of research and started learning about Pets As Therapy dogs. The dogs involved were typically sweet-natured, had good temperaments and a natural way with people or children who were a bit frightened or needed extra support. I booked Maisy for an assessment, and on the evening in question, I planned our car journey to allow a half-hour walk before the test so she'd get the energy she'd built up in the car out of her system beforehand. Things went awry when a thunderstorm struck before the test and we were cooped up in the car for the half-hour preceding the assessment. When we entered the hall, I could only hope that Maisy would do me proud.

The testing was vigorous and involved walking well on the lead and coming to heel on command as many times as necessary. Maisy had to be groomed all over to show she was happy about being touched anywhere on her body. She was subjected to loud crashes and bangs, and didn't react at all. I was also asked to pick her up suddenly and she just looked at me happily, thinking I was giving her a cuddle. I was delighted to be informed we had passed with flying colours.

After Maisy had been registered as an approved PAT dog, the regional coordinator called me and we discussed the list of local places that had put in a request for a dog like Maisy to visit. I already volunteered at a prison with the Shannon Trust, helping the inmates learn to read or to improve their reading level, so when I was asked if I'd be interested in taking Maisy to a prison environment, I said, 'No problem.'

I learnt there was a closed unit nearby – it was run by the NHS – for eleven men who had been convicted of various offences and had complex special needs. Several of them had learning and reading difficulties and I felt that, regardless of their crimes, I wanted to help them with their rehabilitation and, in turn, the wider community by giving the men skills that might make them more productive members of society on their release. The unit was looking for a PAT dog for one afternoon a week to help the men in tandem with the therapies and support they received. I knew Maisy and I would be a perfect fit.

It took four months to get clearance, but eventually we were allowed in for our first visit. When we arrived, most of the men were delighted to see us. One inmate was dog-phobic, so he stayed away, but the others looked forward to our sessions. They baked liver treats for Maisy and learnt to interact with her by doing some obedience work with her in exchange for treats. Every week, I learnt a little more about the group. One member showed me an envelope filled with pictures of his dog. 'I miss him very much,' he said. When he'd been convicted, his parents had taken on his dog until it had become too much for them and they had been forced to give it to a rescue centre for rehoming.

Every week, we sat in a circle and talked about many things. One week, a man started a debate about how dogs don't understand human language. Everybody else, including me, disagreed. We decided to put it to the test, so I took Maisy to him on the lead. 'Tell Maisy to sit down.'

'Maisy, sit.' Maisy bounced her bottom down and up again, ready for a treat.

'Tell her sit, stay.'

He did so, and this time Maisy stayed sitting. The man was impressed and lost faith in his theory!

As the sessions wore on, I began to notice a difference in the men. The environment in which they were living, as well as the reasons that had led them there, and their own needs, caused them a lot of stress.

Being around Maisy calmed them. One man came to the group straight from an assessment. He'd just been diagnosed as autistic and was very upset. Maisy sat between us and he stroked her as he talked about how the diagnosis had made him feel. Maisy didn't move a muscle the whole time. After some time, he began to talk about his Jack Russell.

When the men had returned to their rooms, the occupational therapist who had attended said, 'Did you notice the effect Maisy had on him? She calmed him.'

'She seems to have that effect on a lot of people.'

Whenever one of the men was agitated or upset I would ask if they'd like to come and sit with Maisy and stroke her. Sometimes they would talk a lot and pour out their worries; at others they would fall silent and stroke her in an almost trance-like state.

On one visit, I took along the story I had written about Maisy for Sian and left copies with the men. The following week, they all knew it word for word. 'Would you like to add a chapter about Maisy's visits here?' They were very keen.

At our next meeting, they each dictated a line and I wrote it down:

At first Maisy wasn't too sure about being here and it took time for her to know our different personalities. And we were just a little bit nervous.

Behind-the-scenes at Battersea

Frost the Collie was the perfect pet for park ranger Alex and his wife Debbie.

When Frost passed away, the family knew she could never be replaced, but they were able to give puppy Tilly a new home.

Cocker Spaniels Albert and Dolly suffered from a genetic condition
that left them blind from an early age.

When they passed away, owners Laura and Larry found comfort
from scruffy Boris.

Teddy, pictured with owner Sonia, is an ambassador for combatting misconceptions around Staffies, and was even selected to meet the Queen!

Teddy is proof of his breed's sweet nature, and he formed a special bond with Sonia's son Jack when he fell ill.

English Bulldog Marjorie was suffering from a skin condition after years of neglect, but with the help of her new owner found her way back to health.

Marjorie has helped to raise awareness of backstreet breeding and even brushed paws with the Queen.

After an accident, German Shepherd rescue dog Amber found herself back at Battersea for emergency care.

After a touch-and-go time in surgery, Amber began to show signs of recovery.

Walking again thanks to the care of Battersea's team.

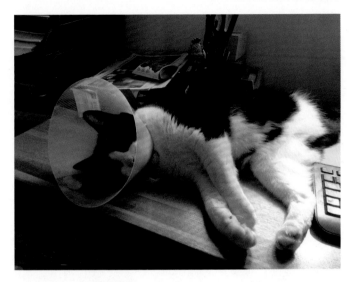

Minty lost a leg in a suspected car accident but went on to make a full recovery.

Minty's family were worried about how she would react to the arrival of their baby, but she proved to be incredibly welcoming.

Now Maisy whimpers when she is in the car because she wants to see her friends.

All of us enjoy Maisy coming because she is a nice dog to make a fuss of and we all love making a fuss of her.

Maisy is ever so quick, as if she doesn't want to miss a trick. She's full of beans and she's always alert. She can sense different smells and different voices and she can sense if someone likes her or not. She can sense if people are happy too.

She can sniff the treats when she comes in through the door and loves the liver cake we made for her. When we give her a treat, her paws go skiddy across the floor.

She's at home with us.

We called their story 'Foreign Territory' and it was a marker of how far the men had come in the months Maisy and I had been visiting. Initially, they had trouble concentrating and it was hard to get them engaged in conversation or tasks with Maisy. Over time, though, they had grown in confidence and learnt how to achieve results with her, how to command her gently but with authority.

After our writing session, one of the men went away and wrote a story about his Staffie, which he'd left behind when he'd been detained. He spent hours writing it, then typed up the final draft and brought it to our session to read aloud. It included a photo of his dog pasted in and we were all moved by his writing. It was later placed in the reception area so that all visitors could see the kind of therapy on offer and the work the men did while they were trying to get their lives back on track. I felt honoured to be a part of their journeys.

I am so thrilled to have taken Maisy in: she has enriched not only our family's life but the lives of everyone she's met and continues to meet, from little Tom to the men in the unit. She's a true gem and I'm immeasurably proud to call her my dog.

Boris the Wonder Dog

My husband and I had just moved our belongings into our new flat but before we even started unpacking, we grabbed the keys, locked the front door and set off for the pet shop. All the time we'd been together, we'd swooned at every single dog we'd seen – it didn't matter to us if it was large or small, black, white, red or brindle. Now that we had our own home, we had to have a dog of our own. I had been lucky enough to grow up with Cairn Terriers, and Larry with Boxers. Now it was open season for what breed we'd end up with.

We arrived at the pet shop and were shown to the puppy enclosure. There, we saw two little Cocker Spaniels, a brother and a sister. She was very excited to see us and bounded over confidently to give us a lick. I could tell she would be the one to get up to mischief. Her brother was cute and chubby and very relaxed.

'What do you think, Laura?'

I told Larry, in no uncertain terms, 'We must have them both.'

We went home with both puppies and named them Dolly and Albert. As we settled in, they did too. Life was blissful until three years later when I noticed that Albert was bumping into things. I took him to the vet and he confirmed that Albert was losing his sight. It was terribly upsetting because he was so young. 'It's a genetic condition called DRSA,' the vet explained, 'and it causes the back of the eye to deteriorate rapidly.'

'Is there anything you can do?'

'I'm afraid not,' he said.

It was then that something dawned on me. 'We have Albert's sister at home. Is she likely to suffer the same problem?'

'Most probably.'

As we talked, I discovered, to my horror, that puppies from pet shops often come from puppy farms where dogs are usually bred under terrible conditions and are much more prone to diseases like this. I vowed never to set foot in a pet shop that sold puppies again.

The vet could see I was very upset about Albert's eyes and tried to reassure me. 'As there are two of them, they will guide each other along. I know what's happening to Albert isn't nice, but you'll be surprised at how well he'll get on with things.'

I hoped he was right.

Life went on, and I fell pregnant. By the time our first baby, Elsie, arrived, Albert had entirely lost his sight and Dolly's was on the way out but, somehow, they muddled along together. We learnt quickly that they moved around the house from memory so if we ever changed the position of the furniture, they'd bump into things. Albert, being the cheeky chap he'd always been, was still very confident and would bound up and down the stairs without any fear. But Dolly became quite nervous. If she did go upstairs, she couldn't come down on her own so we had to carry her. When we held her in our arms, she couldn't tell how high up she was and was nervous of falling.

It was very sad for us to watch the changes in the dogs. We lost so much of the interaction that makes a relationship with a dog so special. A blind dog can't see your eyes and can only rely on your voice. They have no words to tell you how they feel, so when they stop expressing things with their eyes it creates a very different dynamic.

For many years I'd had a vision of having children with Larry and our babies growing up knowing how much fun it is to have a doggy friend. Now, though, Larry and I were carers for our two dogs. Albert and Dolly couldn't see to play fetch or Frisbee, and when we took them to the park, we'd call their names and they'd run towards the sound but never knew exactly where we were.

Nevertheless, Elsie hadn't known Dolly and Albert before they went blind and she loved them dearly. There was lots of stroking and cuddles from all of us but we'd never hear Elsie laughing or giggling as she played with them. Of course, she thought that was how dogs were and never realized that something was missing in her friendship with them. We all loved the dogs, though, and they were a very important part of our family.

One day, a little black cat appeared in our garden and didn't go away. We figured she was a stray and the vet said she was about nine. We started to feed and take care of her. Dolly and Albert knew there was another creature in the house, and if she came close to them, their hackles would go up, but she swanned around as if she owned the place. She quickly worked out that the dogs couldn't see her so she would mosey past them, swishing her tail, until suddenly there was a scatter of paws and all three would dart off in different directions.

Life went on like that until Albert was nine. He had always been chubby, but when one of our friends came over, he remarked that Albert was looking thin. I took a good look at him. Our friend was right. Albert had indeed lost weight. 'I guess we didn't see it because we're with him every day.'

We took Albert to the vet, who said she would run some blood tests.

Just as we were about to leave, I mentioned that Albert had had some swelling next to his tail. The vet examined his anal glands and, almost immediately, looked grave. 'This type of swelling is usually indicative of a particularly aggressive type of cancer. If it's confirmed, he's likely to have a couple of months left. I'm so sorry.'

I was devastated. 'Is there anything you can do? He's still such a young dog.' We discussed our options and she referred us to a specialist vet, who could remove the tumour and give Albert chemotherapy to prolong his life for as long as he was comfortable.

Albert coped remarkably well for a year, but despite the treatment, the cancer spread, and one night he was sick. We knew he was nearing the end, and Dolly could tell too. Usually, the two of them would play and cuddle together but that night she sat with him carefully. It was as if she was afraid to touch him.

The next morning we took Albert to the vet and said our goodbyes. Returning home without him felt surreal. When we came in, Dolly didn't understand why he wasn't with us and kept barking: *Where is my brother?*

Next morning, we told Elsie, who was five now, that Albert had gone to Heaven and was now a star in the sky. She cried a lot, and sometimes went to school sobbing. I, too, often locked myself in the bathroom, crying for Albert, crying for Elsie, crying for Dolly and for us.

It was a heart-breaking time for all of us. Remarkably, though, Dolly seemed to cope better than the rest of us and started playing with the cat.

Then I found out I was three months pregnant. The imminent arrival of a new baby gave us the welcome distraction we needed, and when Nancy arrived, life was back on track.

By now Dolly was going deaf and her legs wobbled a little. At thirteen, she was an old lady, tottering around and snoozing in her bed a lot. As her ailments worsened, I said to Larry, 'If one more thing goes wrong with her, it'll be time for a trip to the vet.'

Recently, we hadn't wanted to take her to the surgery for every little thing because she found it stressful, but, soon enough, she developed an ear infection and we had to go. They put her under a general anaesthetic and cleaned out her ears, but when we brought her home, she wasn't right. She cried all night, and it was clear her ear was really hurting her.

We returned to the vet, who gave her painkillers. 'There might be more to this than an ear infection.'

Larry and I were in agreement that we didn't want to put Dolly through any surgery or more procedures. When the painkillers didn't work, we made a difficult decision. I broke the news to Elsie, who was nine. I held her hands as I explained that Dolly had had enough. 'She's in pain and she's been crying all night. We need to take her to the vet and ask him to put her to sleep so she isn't suffering any more.'

Elsie cried and cried. Then she said, 'Mum, I want to be there. Can I come with you?'

'It won't be very nice. Are you sure you want to?'

Elsie was adamant, so I agreed. The next day, it was a sunny Sunday and we sat in the back garden with Dolly for a while before we left for the clinic. We gave her lots of cuddles and said our goodbyes, but it was very hard on all of us, especially Elsie.

Afterwards, the house seemed very empty. There was no dog to chase the cat and no yapping at the front door whenever anybody walked past. Over time, Dolly had become noisy and barked a lot because she hadn't been able to see what was going on. We missed her very much and Elsie was inconsolable. She'd suffered two big losses in her life and she was only young. Her schoolwork was affected and her demeanour changed as well. Nancy was only four but she missed Dolly as well, asked repeatedly where she had gone and cried because she didn't understand what had happened.

One day, I was clearing up when I found a note on a scrap of paper. I looked closer and recognized Elsie's handwriting. It was a poem she'd written.

> Mummy and Daddy
> Don't be sad
> Albi has gone to Heaven
> If you see two stars in the sky
> It will be Albert and Dolly playing together

I took it to Larry, tears pouring down my face. 'The kids need a dog, Larry, and so do I.' I hated not having a dog to follow me around the house, and I knew Elsie felt the same. Larry worked away a lot and I had come to rely on the noise and chaos the dogs created. At times, too, it was scary when he wasn't at home and the dogs had given me peace of mind. Now, every creak and groan of our house set me on edge. It was true that Dolly had been blind and losing her hearing, but she had always made so much noise that I'd reckoned a burglar would think twice about coming in.

'Let's get another dog, then,' Larry said.

I didn't expect to feel the same towards any other dog as I'd felt for Dolly and Albert, but there were so many dogs out there who needed a home. 'I think we should get a rescue dog this time. We could give it such a great life.'

We were in agreement, so I began my research. I didn't tell Elsie my plan as I didn't want to get her hopes up. Instead, I called my friend David Gandy, the model. He was an ambassador for Battersea and he was so delighted to hear we were thinking of taking on a dog from the Home. 'Oh, Laura,' he said, 'it really is good that you're thinking about rehoming from Battersea.' We talked some more and then he said, 'Why don't you go down and have a look? You'll love it.'

He put us in touch with one of the rehomers, Mary, and we had an interview as a family. We agreed that our needs were quite specific. We had two children, an old cat, and Nancy was asthmatic. We were hoping for a small dog, perhaps a Poodle cross. By now we were living in a bigger house in

Essex and had plenty of room. Mary sent a number of possible matches through but they were all bigger dogs than I had hoped for, or not quite right for us. Then one day I was checking my emails when a picture came through and my heart skipped a beat. The dog in the picture was a curly-haired Labradoodle – a cross between a Labrador and a Poodle – with his paws out and his bottom parked on somebody's lap. His name was Berry and, my word, he was lovely!

I forwarded the picture to Larry, then called his mobile non-stop. 'Larry!' I said, when he finally answered. 'I've found our dog. Quick, check your emails.'

Larry was quiet while he found the email. Then he said, 'He's a bit big, isn't he?'

I didn't care. Berry was gorgeous and his soft eyes told me everything I needed to know about him. He had crazy curls and looked like Boris Johnson. He was practically dripping with personality. I said: 'I've fallen in love with him, Larry.'

He began to laugh. 'He is adorable, isn't he?'

He agreed to call Mary, and that Sunday, I woke the girls up and told them we were going to see a new dog. They couldn't contain their excitement as we piled into my Mini and drove to Battersea. Elsie asked a million questions. 'What's his name? How old is he? What's his breed? What's he like? Is he big? What colour is he?'

I told Elsie all I knew of Berry. 'We'll know more when we arrive and get to meet him.'

The next question was: 'Are we nearly there yet?'

We'd heard our friend David talk so much about the Home and we all loved watching *Paul O'Grady: For the Love of Dogs*, so we were very excited to be seeing Battersea for ourselves. We arrived and were taken through security, then talked to a lady in Reception. We were expected, so she asked us to wait while someone fetched Berry. In the distance, the Thames glistened beyond the Home, and on the opposite bank, the buildings towered high. From certain angles, you could see Battersea Power Station.

The Home itself was a sight to behold. Everywhere you looked, handlers were walking dogs, or carrying cat carriers from one place to another. The famous blue T-shirts we'd seen on staff so many times on the telly were right in front of us now. Battersea Dogs & Cats Home was every bit as amazing as we'd all imagined it to be.

Suddenly Elsie gasped. 'Mum, look! Here he is! It's Berry!'

A lady was walking towards us holding a lead. At the other end, we saw a furry white bundle with long legs and even longer ears. His tail was going like crazy and he looked very happy to see us. The girls were beside themselves and I had to stop them running over to Berry. He looked like a giant teddy-bear. His eyes were sparkling and my heart was racing as he licked our hands and sniffed every bit of us that he could get his nose around. He wanted hugs and stroking and was a gorgeous boy with the personality to match.

'Shall we go for a walk?' the rehomer asked. Elsie and I took it in turns to hold Berry's lead. Nancy was only four so we made sure she didn't trip up or get run over in one of Berry's excited leaps forward. As we walked, the rehomer told us more about him. A couple of months earlier, his owner had dropped him off at a rescue centre in Middlesex. He'd apparently proved to be too much hard work for her and she'd given up on him. He'd later been sent to Battersea in the hope they could rehome him. As I looked at him now, I wondered how on earth anybody could give up on him. He was as lovable as they come. The rehomer explained that Berry had been fostered by a TV personality for the last three weeks. Had it not been for her busy work schedule, she would have kept him.

We learnt that Berry was only ten months old and the knowledge that the foster-mum had fallen in love with him was a good omen. Any worries I might have had melted away. Then Elsie turned to me. 'Can we have him, Mum?'

Elsie

I looked at Mum and thought I would burst. Why was she taking so long to answer? She and Dad smiled and the other lady said, 'If your parents are happy, we're happy for Berry to come home with you.'

I jumped a mile high and punched the sky! For the next hour, or maybe it was longer, I don't remember, the grown-ups did all the boring things they needed to do. All I wanted to do was take Berry home and play with him in the park. When we finally piled into the car, he scooted from one side of the car to the other. He was so fluffy he looked like he'd just got out of the bath, and every time his tail tickled my nose, I giggled. What would he look like after he had actually had a bath? Berry moved from me to Nancy and back again, setting off another round of giggles, this time from my sister. I knew he was going to be lots of fun.

Mum and Dad got into the front. 'Who fancies a burger?'

'*Me! Me!*' Nancy and I shouted, and Berry barked.

We set off, and as the road whizzed by, Berry looked out of the window. I wondered what he was staring at. Dolly and Albie had never done that.

We arrived at the burger restaurant and a few minutes later, our dinner arrived. I had chicken nuggets and so did Nancy. Berry's eyes were as big as saucers and his nostrils were flaring, like a dragon's. Then his mouth flapped open and his big pink tongue rolled out. Berry kept licking his lips. 'Mum! Can I give Berry a chicken nugget?' She said yes so I held one between my fingers and reached out to Berry. 'Here—' Chomp! It was gone before I could even say his name! That set us all off and my sides were aching with laughing, like when Dad tickled me.

Nancy looked at me and scrunched up her nose. She only ever did that when something was really funny. I knew going home with Berry was going to be the best thing ever!

For the rest of the journey, we talked about his name. Then Mum said, 'What about Boris? Like Boris Johnson.'

Dad burst out laughing.

'Who's that?' I asked, which seemed to make Mum and Dad laugh more. Eventually, they explained he was the Mayor of London, had white-blond hair and was known all over the world for his personality.

I looked at Berry and he tilted his head. Well, I guess he did *sort of* look like a Boris. When we got home, Boris ran around the house. He was a maniac! He darted this way and that way, sniffing and bouncing around. He was so different from Dolly and Albie. Those two hadn't known where they were going and didn't really run around. Boris, on the other hand, was leaping about.

After a while he settled down to have a nap, and when he closed his eyes, it was as if a white curtain had come across his face. His hair was long and shaggy and he was funny-looking. We hadn't had him for a day yet but I loved him.

In the morning I went to school and told my friends about my new dog, Boris. They wanted to hear all about him and I was the talk of the class.

I couldn't wait for them to meet him. I told them: 'Maybe you can come round and play with him some time.'

After school, Mum picked me up with Nancy in the car and we rushed home to Boris. When Mum unlocked the door he raced up to see us. *Woof! Woof, woof!* It was as if Boris was saying, *Hello, Mum, hello, Elsie, hello, Nancy!*

Since Dolly had gone to Heaven the house had been so quiet. There was nobody to greet me when I got in from school and that had made me very sad. I'd missed the way Dolly recognized my smell and barked for me to find her for cuddles.

Now, though, gosh, our house was absolutely full of noise! When I arrived home Boris would jump up and plant his paws on my chest. Before I could stop him, his pink tongue had gone LICK! Right up my face. No matter how bad my day at school had been, the moment I saw Boris everything felt better. He was so good at being cuddled, and if we went into the garden, he'd play and play and play. He very quickly became my best friend. He gave us so much love and I wanted him to know how much we loved him too.

Then I had an idea. For three weeks, I saved my pocket money, then asked Mum to take me to the toy shop near our house. I didn't know exactly what I was looking for until I saw a brown woolly lamb. I reached for it. 'Mum, that's it!'

'It's just like the one Dolly had.'

I nodded. Dolly had had a lamb toy just like it, except hers had been blue with a pink face. I took the brown one home to Boris and he absolutely loved it. Instead of ripping it to shreds, like every other toy he had, he carried it around in his mouth, or hid it in his bed.

Boris was as funny as I'd thought he would be. He was massive but he thought he was a little Chihuahua. Whenever I sat on the sofa, he didn't lie by my feet. Instead, he climbed onto the sofa, then onto me! He ran around like a mad dog and every now and then he'd send something flying, which made us all shout, '*Oh, Boris!*'

Sometimes Nancy or I went flying because he'd forget we're only little and not as strong as Mum or Dad.

He got up to so much mischief. One time he dug up a red ant hill and came in covered with ants. We all screamed and shrieked and didn't know what to do while Boris sat in the kitchen, looking very pleased with himself. Another time, he turned himself green by doing roly-polys in the grass Dad had just cut. We had to wash him in the bath.

He wasn't all silly, though. Boris was a really good spider-catcher and soon learnt I was scared of them. Whenever I let out a shriek he'd come running and I'd point to it. 'Boris, look at that!' His nose would go *snuffle, snuffle, snuffle* around my room until he found the spider and barked till Dad put it outside.

He was very good with my little sister too. She hadn't understood where Dolly had gone but she had missed her. When Dolly had been around, they'd sit together and I hated hearing her cry for Dolly after she went to Heaven. But Boris made her giggle. She liked to sit on the floor, and whenever she did, Boris tried to sit on her lap, even though she was little and he was gigantic! When he did manage it, all you could see was a head and a pair of feet from under all Boris's fluff.

When it was Nancy's birthday she asked for a pet of her own. Mum and Dad got her two mice. Boris couldn't believe his eyes when he saw them! He went right up to their cage and stared at them for what seemed like hours! It made us all laugh. What a loon Boris was! My favourite thing about him, though, was how cuddly he was. Nancy's favourites were his wavy tail and floppy ears.

We weren't his only friends, though. Boris had fans everywhere! My friends loved coming over to see him, and whenever they left their bikes in the garden, Boris liked to steal their helmets and, boy, was he fast! Sometimes it was impossible to catch up with him and get things back!

Usually Mum, Nancy and I watched *Paul O'Grady: For the Love of Dogs* together. Boris watched it, too, and I was sure that he recognized people sometimes, because suddenly he'd start to bark his head off.

Now we've had Boris for a year and a bit and I couldn't imagine having any other dog. I miss Dolly and Albie, of course, and whenever I look up to at the sky, I search for the brightest two stars because I know that's them up there. I think they're looking down on us now and thinking, *Thank goodness we don't have to live with that Boris!* He is so loud he would have frightened them. They might even have thought he was a monster because he's big and hairy. But Boris is our monster. A monster that came along and filled the hole in our hearts.

Back from the Brink

The rumbling of our engines broke the Saturday-morning quiet but the faces before us were beaming with excitement. My wife, Jane, and I were part of a group of Harley Davidson motorcyclists, and every weekend around sixty of us got together for special road trips. This one was no exception. We had just arrived at a children's hospice to give a little boy a unique birthday present at the request of his mother. He was too ill to come outside but I could see him standing at a window, waving frantically. We turned off our engines and a few of us went inside to take him a motorcycle-themed birthday cake we'd brought along. He asked us lots of questions and we signed his pyjamas with a message. He was chuffed to bits to see us and we were pleased to have helped give him such a great surprise.

Our charity work and motorcycles were just some of the ways Jane and I kept ourselves busy. During the week, I worked as a long-distance driver, delivering supplies to homeware stores around the country. Sometimes I did night shifts, and with Jane working during the day, we were like ships that passed in the night. But we'd been married for sixteen years and were a happy team because we talked out any problems. We didn't have any children and our conversations would often turn to the same topic: 'Wouldn't it be amazing if we could have a dog, John?' Jane would say.

'If only we had the time to take care of one.'

Jane had grown up with Dobermans, and I'd always had German Shepherds when I'd lived with my family, so we were fans of big dogs. But the timing and our life-style were never quite right for us to realize our dream. We put it on the back-burner and life ploughed on.

One icy winter morning I was making a delivery up north when I had an accident unloading the trailer. I felt a sharp pain in my back so I reported it in the work accident log. When I was driving home, the pain became excruciating. It was as if my spine was being crushed.

Jane took me to Northampton Hospital. I could no longer walk and had to be pushed in a wheelchair. Despite my symptoms and terrible pain, the X-ray and MRI scans showed no damage. My condition baffled consultants because the pain I was suffering was unbearable. I was given test after test, injections, epidurals and steroids into my spine, but nothing worked. I moved around on crutches and didn't leave the house except to go to the hospital or the doctor's surgery. I was forced to quit my job, and with Jane working to keep us afloat, my days became very isolated. Our parents were elderly and did their best to pop in during the day and make me a sandwich, but it was hard on everyone. I was unable to lift the kettle without shouting in pain, so the best I could do was take a cocktail of painkillers and go to bed. When I was awake, the pain medication made me drowsy. As time passed, I began to feel very depressed.

That wasn't surprising. I had been forced to give up everything I loved – my job, my motorcycle and my freedom. I was a prisoner in my home, and I was worried about Jane. She was working so hard for both of us and I could see how exhausted she was.

We'd been together for twenty-two years, married for twenty-one, and the thought of dragging her down or making her sad was dreadful. When we'd first become a couple, we'd both come out of bad relationships so we'd vowed never to make each other unhappy. We'd promised to talk to each other and never bottle things up. I realized it was time for me to re-affirm that promise by telling her the truth now.

'You should leave me and find yourself somebody new.'

Jane was so taken aback that her eyes instantly filled with tears. 'Don't be stupid, John! Why would I ever want anybody else?'

'You'd be better off without me and all my problems,' I said.

Jane put her arms around me and held me tightly. I hugged her back, though I couldn't understand why she would want to comfort and stay with me. I had nothing to offer her now, except misery and pain. At times I had wondered if everybody would be better off if I wasn't around. I was suffering extreme pain daily with no explanation or hope that it would ever stop. When I told her that, she made me promise never to do anything stupid.

'I'm not going anywhere, John, so please talk to me when you're feeling like this.'

With Jane's support I returned to the doctor once more and asked for another opinion. Time passed and, finally, the doctors were able to give me a diagnosis. I was suffering from complex regional pain syndrome, likely to have been triggered by the accident at work. It explained my symptoms. It was a relief to have some answers, even if it meant the outlook remained the same. There was no known cure for CRPS and, in some cases, time was the only effective healer. My condition was probably there to stay. My pain levels were not showing any improvement but knowing what I was suffering with helped me cope better emotionally.

Jane and I discussed the diagnosis and concluded that my life, our life together, was unlikely to go back to the way it had been. I doubted I'd ever be able to ride a Harley again or spend hours on the road, or move from one hospital to the next doing charity work. I'd certainly not go back to full-time work.

But that didn't mean we couldn't or shouldn't start thinking about our future. Then Jane had an idea. 'Why don't we get a dog now? You're at home all the time and you need some company. It will do you the world of good.'

I loved the idea, but . . . 'I don't think it will be fair on the dog. I can't do anything like take it for walks or play with it.'

'Maybe we can think about it again in a few months' time.'

Armed with my new diagnosis, I attended a pain management clinic where the specialist looked at all my medications and came up with a tweaked plan to see if it improved things. It did, and over time, I started to feel a bit more mobile and independent. I was able to drive again, which made me feel a sense of renewed freedom and helped with the depression.

I thought back to Jane's idea of getting a dog. At least now I was able to drive I could take a dog to the park. I loved animals so much that I'd never consider getting one if I wasn't able to give it the good life it deserved. I didn't want to take a rescue dog out of kennels only to keep it cooped up in the house with just me for company. But finally, after years of pain, I felt in control once more, so I told Jane what I was thinking.

'Oh, John, that would be wonderful.'

Jane and I started looking online to find out what our options were, beginning with local rescue centres. Then, we turned our attention to Battersea Dogs & Cats Home. Initially, I was very interested in the Husky dogs.

We continued our search over several weeks, me on the desktop computer in the kitchen, and Jane on her laptop. There was one dog on the Battersea site that I kept coming back to. When Jane came in to make a cup of tea, I told her about it.

'It's not Bubbles, the American Bulldog, is it?'

My jaw dropped. 'Yes!' It turned out we'd both been looking at Bubbles's profile and something about her was drawing us in. 'I think I'd like to meet her.'

'Me too,' Jane said.

We gave Battersea a call and arranged to go to Old Windsor to see Bubbles. Before we went, we made sure to do lots of reading up on the American Bulldog breed so that we could have a grasp of what to expect if we were to rehome Bubbles. We learnt they are very stubborn and can become transfixed with certain things, like licking their feet and making them sore. We read forums and American Bulldog websites, watched videos on YouTube and read breeder testimonials. The dogs grew large, needed exercise, like most dogs, but liked to sleep a lot too. They were people-friendly and often known as nanny dogs for their patient and gentle manner with children. Every single forum poster confirmed the same thing: that American Bulldogs made great pets and provided gold-class friendship for young and old. Jane and I agreed that Bubbles sounded perfect for us.

That weekend, we made the seventy-mile drive to Old Windsor. There, we were shown to a room and a big dog was brought in. The rehomer wanted to see how we'd handle it before we were taken to meet

Bubbles. This American Bulldog was quite hyper and jumping all over the place but, within a few minutes, we'd managed to calm him down and he sat beside us for some strokes and treats. The rehoming team were impressed with our skill in handling a dog of his size. Next, we were taken to a room with chairs and a big box of dog toys in the corner.

The rehomer brought Bubbles in and she seemed a bit nervous so we stayed seated. When Bubbles went past us to sniff around the room, we tentatively gave her a stroke. She was a beautiful white with a gorgeous black patch over her right eye. On her loop back, she came to us and we were able to stroke her properly, then throw a ball for her. She responded well.

'Can we take her for a walk?' Jane asked.

'Of course,' the rehomer said. 'Take as long as you want and let us know your thoughts when you're done.'

We clipped on her lead and took a stroll around Battersea Old Windsor's beautiful grounds. Bubbles pulled on her lead a bit and I made a mental note that we'd need to train her out of doing that.

As the walk went on, she began to look at us more and pay us a bit more attention.

Before I knew it, an hour had flown by so we took her to a fenced-in area and let her off the lead. We threw the ball for her and every time she returned it to me, and we were able to look each other in the eye, I felt our bond strengthening. 'What do you think, Jane?'

'I like her a lot.'

I took the plunge. 'I'd like to take Bubbles home with us.'

Jane smiled. 'Me too.'

We returned to speak to the rehomer and learn more about Bubbles's background. She was eleven months old and had been returned to the home four times through no fault of her own. The first owner had developed asthma, the second found out she was pregnant a week after getting Bubbles . . . The list of reasons went on and it seemed Bubbles had experienced a run of bad luck.

We filled out the paperwork, and as Bubbles had been microchipped, spayed and had had her injections, we were able to take her home with us that day. We were given a free box of food, a Battersea lead and collar, plus free pet insurance for a month. It was everything we needed to get started.

Bubbles turned out to be scared of loud noises, and if you moved too quickly, she'd get a bit frightened. She was wary of her bowl, too, and would wait till you'd put it down and stepped quite far back before she began eating. She was scared of going up the stairs and I wondered what had happened to her to make her so anxious. We set up her bed underneath the stairs so that she felt secure but wasn't hemmed in.

Next day, Jane set off to work and it was just me and Bubbles. She followed me around the house and we played with her ball. I took her for a walk and when we came home, we were both so worn out we had a nap. When I woke up, I was surprised to see that it was nearly time for Jane to get home. Soon she arrived, eager to hear how our first day alone had gone.

'For the first time since my accident, the time whizzed by.'

'I'm so pleased, John.'

Over the days and weeks that followed, Bubbles began to settle in and was happy to roam around the house on her own. Her true personality began to shine through as her anxiety melted away.

I learnt she was terrible at recall, food-oriented, would sit to command, and if you went out of the room for five minutes, she'd behave as though you'd been away for a week when you came back. Bubbles was excitable, loving, affectionate and a joy to have around. She was quiet unless someone was at the door or we were playing tug-of-war with her rope toy. And she could sleep for England.

But it seemed that Bubbles wasn't the only one who was changing. Jane noticed that my attitude was different and I wasn't so down any more. 'You've got that sparkle in your eye back and you're laughing again.' She was right. In the time following my accident, I couldn't see the funny side of anything and had literally stopped laughing. 'I'm getting my John back,' she added.

It was really good to see Jane happy again. Throughout the length of our marriage, we'd had only one argument, early on, and that had been entirely my fault. I'd learnt over the years that Jane knew me better than I knew myself. Her suggestion of getting a dog was the best idea she'd ever had and I wouldn't have been bold or brave enough to do it of my own accord.

At the weekends, we drove to the woods nearby and we clipped Bubbles to a thirty-foot training lead so that I could keep hold of her while I stayed by the car and watched her play and run around. It was a way for the three of us to enjoy a day together without me getting exhausted. After I'd had enough, I'd get back into the car while Jane wandered off with Bubbles. Over time, my tolerance for walking improved and I was able to get by with just one crutch for longer and longer. As Bubbles exercised and gained muscle, I exercised with her and gained stamina. We were good for each other and my journey back to health was a team effort.

Bubbles steadily gained weight until she weighed forty kilos. She was a very big girl with a heart of gold. Whenever she sensed I was having a bad day, she stayed by my side and wouldn't leave me for a second. On days when I was better she'd meander into another room and come in every now and then to check on me.

She had her cheeky side too. Whenever she didn't want to do something Jane told her to, she'd run to her daddy for protection. I understood why. We spent so much time together and I did lots of training with her. I put in all the hours because I wanted to, and also because Bubbles was extremely stubborn. Training her was a mammoth task. But I persevered and took Bubbles into the garden every day. Eventually, she learnt to sit, give me her paw, walk to heel, lie down and do a high five. It took a lot of patience because sometimes, if Bubbles wasn't in the mood, she wouldn't play along at all. Other days, she was amazing and did everything I asked of her. It was impossible to get bored with her around and I no longer watched the clock as I had when I was on my own.

The only thing I wasn't able to conquer was Bubbles's excitement at meeting people or jumping up when she saw somebody she loved. She had a habit of getting up on her back legs and resting her big paws on your shoulders while licking you half to death.

By the time she was nearly three, Bubbles had become used to me being around, so when I went to the hospital and left her alone, I felt guilty. 'What do you think about getting Bubbie a companion?' I asked Jane.

She raised her eyebrows, then grinned. 'It would be nice for her to have company when we're both out of the house.'

We began a new search. We were careful when considering our options because Bubbles was a big dog and extremely playful. Some dogs were intimidated by her. I'd seen it many times in the park when Bubbles had raced over to another dog to say, *How do you do?*, tail wagging fast, but the other dog had been spooked and tried to bite her. She was too big to approach other dogs without freaking them out and she had come to realize that they were prone to nipping her. At the beginning, she hadn't expected that and had always run back to me, shaking and scared. As she'd wised up to their behaviour, she had learnt to handle them on her own. She would simply hold the animal down so it couldn't bite her until its owner arrived to take it away. My Bubbles knew not to bite or attack other animals, and it made me cross when some owners wouldn't take responsibility for their dog.

We had to make sure that the dog we brought in to keep Bubbles company was not only well matched with her but also that Bubbles liked it.

We contacted Bullies In Need and talked to a lady there who asked us about our situation and about Bubbles. 'I have a Staffie not too far from your home. He's actually an American Bulldog Staffie cross, and he's a beefy dog who can hold his own. Maybe he's the right fit for Bubbles.'

We were told Duke had suffered a seizure and his previous owner had handed him over to the rescue centre, unwilling to take on any medical issues he might have been developing. I felt sorry for him. Whatever problems he was having with his health, he deserved a good home with owners who would love him no matter what. His being abandoned made me think back to my darkest times. What if Jane had given up on me like that? I knew I had to see Duke. 'Can we meet him?'

'Before you do, you need to know that Duke doesn't like to share his toys and is quite possessive of them.

But he doesn't have any problems with sharing food.' That was good to know.

We made our arrangements, and the following week, we took Bubbles to meet him. They had a sniff and a bit of a grumble at each other, but as we got talking, they settled down and began running around after each other. He was just under a year old and was yet to be neutered, but other than that, things were looking promising. Bubbles and Duke played happily together, and, once they were tired, ended up sitting next to each other, staring at us. They were like two peas in a pod. It wasn't a concern that they'd had a bit of a grumble at each other when they'd first met because, like we humans, dogs need a bit of time to size each other up and figure out if they like each other or not. Looking at the pair of them now, it was clear they were going to be good friends.

We brought Duke home a week later. He had not suffered any seizures since he'd been at the rescue centre but we kept a sharp eye on him just in case. We took him to our vet, who looked him over and couldn't see any problems. 'Sometimes seizures happen. Look out for tremors.'

We noticed a few episodes of tremors and Duke shaking his head but it stopped altogether before long. Perhaps it had been brought on by stress. We were never going to find out.

Bubbles loved having him around and now I was second fiddle. It didn't bother me, though, because the house was full of noise, and with the pair of them to look after, Jane and I were kept on our toes. If I was having a bad day, Jane would take each of them out in turn. They were strong, heavy dogs, and taking them out together was too much of a task sometimes. If one of them was out, the other would whine and pine until they returned home.

During the day, I began training Duke as I had Bubbles. He was much easier to train because he wasn't half as stubborn. But he did have a habit of pushing Bubbles around, which she tolerated. Whenever she was chewing something Duke wanted, he'd take it from her, then she'd come into the kitchen, where we'd inevitably be, and whine until we got it back for her, whatever the item was. Overall, however, they were a good fit. Bubbles wasn't interested in toys and Duke liked to hoard his. Bubbles liked humans, and he liked dogs. He had ninja hearing, and whenever I was in the kitchen and lifted the lid of the biscuit tin, he'd run in and stare at me until I gave him a piece.

He knew when Jane's usual bedtime was, and if she left it half an hour late, he'd bark at her until she put her pyjamas on. He was as good as a watch, that dog. We both knew that Duke was a mummy's boy and Bubbles was a daddy's girl, but we loved the pair of them as though they were our children, and in return they loved us back with absolute dedication and loyalty. If Bubbles wanted to climb under the covers with

Jane, and Duke wanted to carry on playing with me downstairs, their loyalties would very conveniently flip.

One evening, I was in the kitchen when I started to feel a bit funny. Just as I was about to call for Jane, things went black. When I came to, I didn't have the strength to call out for her so I told Duke, who was hovering anxiously next to me, 'Dukey, go and get Mummy. Go get Mummy.'

He ran upstairs and barked and barked until Jane came down and found me on the kitchen floor. She was able to help me up and once I was sitting comfortably we tried to figure out what had happened. We reckoned that because I didn't sleep very well, the tiredness from my insomnia had caused me to pass out. It was lucky that Duke had been in the kitchen with me that night, because if Bubbles had been in one of her stubborn moods, and I'd asked her to get Jane, she would have looked at me with an expression that said: *Get her yourself!* Duke was much more obliging.

The dogs are endlessly entertaining and really are our best friends. Now, our house is full of laughter, something that, just a few years ago, I couldn't have imagined would be the case. For so long after my accident, my home was my cage. With Bubbles first, and later Duke, I got my freedom back. My pain may never entirely go away, but with Jane and the dogs at my side, I have an excellent quality of life. That is priceless.

Her Royal Marjesty

I left the lecture hall, and as my classmates piled outside for lunch, I turned in the opposite direction and moved quickly towards the halls of residence. I went into my room, climbed into bed and pulled the covers over my head. I wasn't enjoying my course and, if I was honest with myself, I wasn't settling in. Four months had passed since I'd started at the university, and I felt alone and miserable. That night, I called home and my mum, Amanda, answered. As soon as she heard my voice, she said, 'What's wrong, Hollie?'

I took a big breath and it all came pouring out. 'I think I want to come home, Mum. For good.'

'Whatever makes you happy, darling.'

I quit my sport-science degree and returned to my parents' home in South London. It should have been a relief but I felt deflated. I hid myself away for a few months, unsure what to do next and anxious about what the future held. Every day I took our West Highland White Terrier, Millie, to the park to try to shake off the cabin fever, but she was old and wasn't interested in staying out for long. Then I had an idea. 'Mum, please may I have my own dog?'

Mum wasn't keen. 'Millie's too old to share her space with another dog. It wouldn't be fair on her now.'

I understood where she was coming from, and I wanted what was best for Millie too, so I put the idea to the back of my mind.

Time passed. I heard what my friends were up to, and about the adventures my twin sister, Imogen, was having, travelling the world, and felt at odds with myself. I was twenty-one: shouldn't I be doing something with my life? I'd start thinking about getting a job, which made me even more anxious. It was a vicious cycle.

Then Millie passed away from old age, and we were all very upset. She'd been around for as long as I could remember and now, suddenly, she was gone. I was doing the odd babysitting job but little else, which left me with a lot of time to think about Millie, how much I missed her and how empty my life felt.

Then an opportunity arose to pull me out of myself. Mum's friend, whom she'd known for years through walking Millie, told Mum she was a kennel volunteer at Battersea Dogs & Cats Home. 'She says they run a fostering scheme,' Mum told me. 'You can take in cats and dogs that need time out of kennels until they find a for-ever home.'

The more I heard about becoming a foster carer for Battersea, the more excited I became. That was what

I needed to do. It meant I'd have the joy of helping a dog without committing to take care of it for ever. It would give me direction without putting me under too much pressure. Perfect.

When I called Battersea, I learnt that their fostering programme was in its infancy and only two other volunteers were involved. I talked to the lady for some time, and she arranged for someone from Battersea to come to my home and check it was suitable for dogs.

A few days went by, and a woman came to visit us from the Home. She made sure we had enough space and that the garden was safe for a dog. 'Why do you want to do this?' she asked.

I thought about it for a moment. 'I can't afford to have a dog but I have the time and the space to help one get back on its feet.' I had already filled out my application form so I handed it to her and off she went.

After a month without any news, I chased up the relevant office and left a message. About an hour later, my phone rang. I answered, and Kerry from Battersea said, 'Are you free tomorrow? We have a dog that would do really well as a foster.'

I made arrangements to go to Battersea, but as the evening wore on, I realized that after Millie had passed away, we'd given away anything dog-related. I emailed Kerry in a panic and she answered: *Don't worry, we'll give you everything you need.* What a relief!

Next day, I went to the Home and waited in Reception for Kerry. She appeared with a black Staffordshire Bull

Terrier at the end of her lead. Lily was unbelievably thin and, for a dog of only two, she looked very old indeed. Lily had been used for breeding, then dumped on the street after she'd had her latest litter. Her mammary glands were swollen and her stomach distended. It was clear she'd only recently had the puppies. The sight of her made me want to cry because, despite her ordeal, she was so excited to see everyone.

Her tail was wagging and her bum was wiggling as she looked at this person, then that person, with eyes that said, *Hello, everybody!*

I spoke to the vet, who told me Lily was very underweight at fifteen kilos. She needed to be above twenty and would need two hundred grams of food three times a day and limited walks so she didn't burn too much energy as we tried to build her up. Then Kerry helped me load my car with blankets, bedding, food and, finally, Lily. She wouldn't stay in the boot as she was too excited so I put her in the front with me. She sat down as if she'd always been there. I snapped a picture of her as a keepsake, a fresh start for both of us.

Lily had to be walked and fed, and I was responsible for both. It was wonderful having someone who was reliant on me because it meant my own worries had to wait. After a few days' acclimatizing, I began to send foster reports, telling the Home how Lily was doing, how she was coping with being handled, when she liked to eat, where she slept and if she had settled. I also wrote a little piece about her personality to go on the website profile to help prospective owners get to know her a bit.

Lily is a sweet, happy-go-lucky lady, who needs someone to give her the care and attention she deserves so that she can learn how to socialize again and reconnect with the world around her.

Every Saturday morning, I dropped Lily off at Battersea so that potential owners could meet her. Then I'd wait by the phone until four o'clock to learn whether or not she had been chosen by a family.

One Saturday, four weeks after Lily had come to stay, I had that call. I listened to the rehomer, who told me that a family had reserved Lily and would be making a decision on whether or not to go ahead the following day. I thought, Oh, no! I don't want to let her go. By now, Lily had settled in, gained weight and was growing attached to me. The same was true in reverse, and I felt quite attached to Lily.

But I knew that to continue with fostering I had to let Lily go. Next day, the family who had been to visit Lily decided to adopt her and I was given a week to get her ready. I focused on the fact that she was going to a loving home, to a family who would cherish her. The next Saturday, I dropped her off with a heavy heart. As I was walking out of the gates, I saw three dogs being brought in by members of the public to the Lost and Found reception area. 'I found this dog wandering around without a collar near my home,' I heard one say. 'I think it's a stray. Can you help?'

I knew then that I could foster again because, no matter how hard it was for me to let each dog go, the satisfaction I took from knowing it was going to a forever home made it all the more worthwhile. That night, the house was very quiet and I felt quite relieved. I'd done a good job: I had accomplished what I had set out to do with Lily. But when I looked at her empty little bed, I felt a pang of sadness. It was eased, though, with the knowledge that Lily was sleeping in her new bed, in her new home on a beautiful farm in Wales. What a life she would have.

Within a week, I'd picked up my next foster dog, a little Staffie called Richie. He'd been at Battersea longer than Lily, and was eighteen months old with a lot of bad habits. I was warned he needed training to learn to respect boundaries. He stayed with me for two months, and I worked with him to help him understand that it wasn't all right to jump up at people, and that he had to eat his food in the kitchen. It was intense, but every time he made progress, I felt ready to burst with pride. It was very satisfying to know that I was helping shape him into a dog fit for rehoming.

After that, I became a regular fosterer. Many dogs came and went through our home, and with each one, I catered to its different needs. Some were easy to rehome and had been unfortunate victims of circumstance, while others needed a lot of time and effort, then a good match with a future owner: it was very important to ensure that when a dog left the Home, it would be with someone who could continue the level of care it needed.

By the time I got to dog number fifteen, three years on, I was quite experienced and confident in my ability to handle pretty much any dog.

Then a team member at the Home called. 'We've got this dog . . .' Whenever they began like that, I knew I'd be facing a challenge.

The dog, a Labrador cross named Missy, was pregnant, and would need a foster home for the next few months until her pups were born and ready for rehoming. 'Would you be interested in fostering her and potentially birthing her, doing all that that will entail with the puppies?'

I didn't hesitate. 'Yes, that's fine, of course.'

I was still living at home with Mum and Dad but things were going well. I worked a few hours here and there as a nanny, and I was quite happy with the balance in my life. I took Missy on, excited about the months ahead. Battersea sent me lots of information on what to look out for in a dog about to give birth, and what sort of an environment to give her. I prepared a quiet, cosy spot under the stairs so she had some privacy but wasn't isolated from the rest of the house. She arrived two days later with a big belly. I could hear her in the middle of the night, rearranging her bedding and nesting. We didn't know how long it would be until the puppies arrived.

One morning, I was woken by high-pitched squealing. It was five o'clock so I roused Mum and we went down together. There was Missy, nursing a tiny puppy. It was a beautiful sight. But then I noticed a tiny shape further away. It was another puppy, but she hadn't made it. I wrapped her in a blanket and moved her away so Mum didn't become upset.

I sat with Missy, and half an hour later, she began pushing. I had been instructed not to get involved unless Missy was distressed and, soon enough, puppy number three arrived. Hours passed and everything seemed fine until suddenly Missy began to shake from nose to tail. She became very distressed very quickly and was behaving strangely, pushing the puppies away, curling up and whining. I called Battersea and was advised to bring her and the litter in. We set off, and when we arrived at the Home and the vet examined Missy, she found that a fourth puppy was stuck in the birth canal. Missy had to stay in overnight so I returned home, a nervous wreck. That night I didn't sleep a wink, and was back as soon as possible the following morning. Overnight, Missy had given birth to a fifth puppy and I was taken to see her with the puppies that had made it.

The nurse explained Missy was behaving very protectively and wouldn't let anyone near her pups.

'Maybe she'll be OK with you as she knows you,' she added.

Missy looked at me hopefully and let me inside her kennel without any problem. She let me stroke her and the puppies. It must have been a very distressing time for Missy but it was nice that she trusted me. It showed I was doing my job properly.

An hour later, the four of us were on our way home.

When we got there, I was finally able to take a good look at the puppies, two girls and a boy, and they were just gorgeous. It was thought Missy had mated with a French Mastiff and one of the girls was ginger with a white stripe down her face. We named her Kelele, which is Swahili for 'noisy' as she was constantly squeaking. The boy, Loki, was sandy-coloured with a squashed nose and we called him Loki because he was naughty! The second girl was called Lizzie but, sadly, she didn't survive.

For the first few weeks, Missy had to be fed puppy food while the pups were nursing. Then I helped wean them off her milk by feeding them every two hours with puppy food. It was amazing and exhausting but so worthwhile. I had been told to socialize the puppies and let them become used to people while they were still with me, so I texted my friends: *Puppies! We have puppies! Feel free to come and visit!*

They piled in over the next few weeks, and Missy was happy to let people touch, stroke and hold her puppies, while she hovered nearby, but she couldn't tolerate other dogs.

By the time the puppies were ready for rehoming, Mum was very taken with Kelele. 'Do you think we might be able to keep her?'

I thought about it and reckoned we'd be in with a decent chance if that was what we wanted, but in the end, I said, 'I don't think it's best for Missy.' I knew that she was feeling quite fed up with everyone and needed some time to regroup. She'd had a difficult few months and I sensed her head was still spinning with all the change. I had some training to do with her and I wanted to do that without the puppies around.

I made the call to Battersea: 'The puppies are ready to be rehomed.'

There was a long waiting list for puppies so I knew they wouldn't be at Battersea for long. After Kelele and Loki had left, Missy went back to her old easygoing self, with humans and dogs alike.

A few weeks later, she passed her final assessment. This included being observed playing, having her toys and food removed and given back, to identify any possessive tendencies, checking to see if she was happy to be touched and handled, and whether she was able to walk and interact with other dogs. She passed with flying colours and I felt really good about that. Mum had seen all the work I'd put in: 'If you hadn't done it, she might never have found a new home, you know.'

Two days later, and after five months in our home, Missy was on her way to her new owner.

I continued fostering, and had everything from Jack Russells to Staffies. Mum and Dad were retired and very supportive of my passion for dogs and fostering. From time to time we discussed keeping a dog permanently and agreed that when the right one came along we'd make it work. Mum added, 'But it will be your dog, not ours.'

'Agreed,' I said.

Seven years after taking on Lily, my first foster dog, I took stock of my life and saw that it had changed immeasurably. A few years after leaving my degree course, I had taken a part-time job in a local nursery run by Mum's friend and gradually my hours there had increased. I had scaled back my fostering work to short-term stays only, and now I knew what I wanted to do. I gave notice at the nursery and applied for an Open University course to study for the degree that ignited my passion: child psychology. There would be a number of months when I would be at home all the time, starting now, so I sent emails to my fostering contacts at the Home. *I'm back! I'm ready for more! What do you have for me?*

I got chatting to a few members of the team, and then, with my family for moral support as I eased back into things, I went to see Chris, one of the other Battersea foster carers whom I'd become friends with. We were walking her dogs when I said, 'I hear a

Bulldog has arrived at Old Windsor. Do you reckon I could meet her?'

'Of course!' She told me a little about Marjorie, a two-year-old English Bulldog. 'She was found on the street and she's still in a bad way. Are you sure you want to meet her?'

I nodded, and asked Chris to tell me more. Marjorie had full body mange from mites under her skin, which had caused her fur to fall out, and she was underweight. It was clear from her swollen, lactating teats and prolapsed cervix that she had been used repeatedly for backstreet breeding. Her problems indicated that she had had three or four litters. She had crusty, infected eyes, her ears were full of gunk, her skin was raw and pink, and she had painful cysts on her paws. It was heart-breaking to hear how she had been so shamelessly used and abused, then turfed out to fend for herself.

Chris put me in touch with Rachel at Old Windsor, where Mum, Imogen and I arranged to meet Marjorie. We waited in the reception area while Rachel fetched Marjorie, and fifteen minutes later, we were shown to a quiet room away from the hustle, bustle and excitement that always seemed to surround Reception. There, in the corner, was a little cat bed and somehow Marjorie had jammed herself into it. Her teeth stuck out from her lips and she had the cutest coat on to keep her warm in the absence of fur. She was underweight, that much was clear, and she needed the extra layer to stop her shivering.

Mum, Imogen and I looked at each and I knew from their faces that they were thinking the same as I was. Marjorie was the one for us, not as a foster but as a permanent member of our family.

I approached her and sat on the floor next to the bed. Marjorie's tail began to wag, and I held my hand out for her to sniff it. Mum sank down next to me. 'This is it, isn't it, Hollie? Marjorie's the one.'

None of us could explain why but we all felt in our hearts that Marjorie was destined to come home with us. I told Rachel I wanted to foster her for sure, with a view to keeping her, and she said that Marjorie wasn't ready to leave them yet. 'She still needs a lot of medical care but I'll put a note on her file that you will be her foster mum, with a view to permanently adopting when she's better.'

I left Battersea on Cloud Nine. All the years I'd fostered dogs, I had always reminded myself why I was fostering. I'd cherished every moment I had spent taking a dog into my home and into my heart, giving it the care it needed to make it ready for its for-ever home. No matter how sad I was to say goodbye to a dog, I knew that within twenty-four hours there would be another dog that needed love and care. Because of that, I had never come close to rehoming a dog myself: I had always felt another foster dog would need me more. But Marjorie had changed that in our short time together: I knew I simply couldn't give her to someone else.

A few weeks later and Marjorie was ready for fostering, as long as I could bring her back every Friday for her skin to be checked at the clinic. That wasn't a problem, so I went to pick her up and was given a medicated lotion to bathe her in daily and the antibiotics she needed. When I got her home, she spent a lot of time lying down and snoozing. She was overwhelmed, nervous, tired, and needed a bit of time and space to adjust. She had been through so much, from being dumped on the streets to being in kennels and now at home with us. It was a lot for her to take in, so I left her to wander around where and when she wanted to. At night, she'd go to her bed under the stairs. It was one that I'd spent an hour choosing for its super-soft padded foam and white faux-fur lining. I hoped it would help to soothe her irritated skin.

As the weeks passed, Marjorie relaxed into herself and I got to know her. Each day she revealed a new quirk to me. As we became firm friends, I learnt she was the kind of dog that wanted love from everyone she met but she'd stay put wherever she was and look at new friends with eyes that said: *I want your cuddles, but you're going to have to come to me!* Once she got to know you, however, she was all over you. It was impossible for my friends to come in and out of the house without receiving slobbery kisses from Marjorie, especially those she knew well.

Whenever the cleaner came, Marjorie lost the plot. She descended into a frenzy of excitement, giving licks and kisses and demanding hugs. I couldn't understand why Marjorie had such an affinity with her until I saw her slipping Marjorie doggy treats. She had a dog at home and loved Marjorie so much that she brought her a pocketful of treats every time she came to our house. That explained a lot!

One of my most treasured moments with Marjorie was when my friend's French Bulldog puppy, Monty, came to stay with us. The two dogs formed such a bond that Marjorie took Monty into her bed, where the pair spent whole afternoons snuggled up together. It was as if she was taking in a little foster of her own and she fussed around him, licking him as if he were hers. For the ten days that Monty stayed with us, Marjorie played the role of mummy, showing Monty where he had to eat his dinner or where he had to go if he needed a wee. It was both heart-warming and heart-breaking to see her in mummy mode. I would never know how many puppies she'd had taken away from her, but there was no doubt about it: her maternal instinct was very strong.

When it was time for Monty to go home, Marjorie pined for him and I wondered if I had made a mistake in taking him on while his mum went away on holiday. But then Marjorie seemed to get over it and was back to her usual self. She was remarkably resilient and I felt very proud.

As time went on, I came to recognize the things that Marjorie didn't like, such as sudden noises or anything coming close to her face. If we went to a pet shop to pick up some supplies, I had to carry my bag of purchases on the other side from Marjorie's lead because she wouldn't walk next to it. I reckoned she hated the rustling noise. It made me wonder if she'd had some negative experience with bags in her life before us. It was difficult not knowing exactly what had happened to her and having constantly to guess. Sometimes my imagination would run wild and I would get very upset thinking about the lonely and difficult times my beautiful girl had suffered. It was very likely that she had been kept in a room on her own, not fed properly and without veterinary care. She wouldn't have had the correct food when pregnant or shortly after giving birth.

It wasn't surprising, then, that Marjorie was easily spooked. She hated big packages arriving at the house, and while on some days she liked to play with her tennis ball, on others she was scared if you threw it for her. Whenever I did some nanny work, I took Marjorie along and she was quite tolerant, but if things got too noisy or the kids were shouting, her body language spelt out to me loud and clear that she was uncomfortable.

Every day I had to bathe Marjorie in the medicated lotion the Battersea vets had provided and it was really stinky. Marjorie hated it as much as I did, but she patiently waited in the bath while I did what had to be done and, in time, her skin began to improve. It no longer looked pink and raw and her fur grew back, although some scars became visible on her forehead from the months of untreated mite damage before she'd been rescued.

Weeks went by, and I received a call from a member of the Public Affairs team at Battersea. She told me they were starting a new campaign to stop backstreet breeding. Their report into the matter had concluded that of the estimated 560,000 puppies born in England every year, less than 12 per cent of them came from licensed breeders. This meant that all too often the mothers were ill-treated, then abandoned when they were no longer of use. The puppies that survived the terrible environment they were often born into were sold with chronic health or behaviour problems. The shocking lack of regulation in the market enabled breeders to sell those dogs from unsuitable premises long before they were ready to leave their mothers. It was a campaign close to my heart.

I'd seen how much care Missy had needed when she'd given birth, then nursed and weaned her puppies, so it was hard to imagine the kind of experience Marjorie had been through, surviving without love and care when she was at her most vulnerable. I was happy to help Battersea, so when they asked if Marjorie and I would be in the video and social media for the campaign, I didn't hesitate to say yes.

We went along for a photo-shoot and soon the campaign launched. Marjorie and I were interviewed by BBC 5 Live and I told Marjorie's story. I hoped that if people heard what she had been subjected to, it would make them stop to think about the consequences of buying puppies from unlicensed breeders. Marjorie came along to meetings with politicians to encourage them to deal with the regulatory aspects of the campaign, which reached more than 330,000 people.

When the Home's new Mary Tealby intake kennels were due to open after a huge renovation project, Marjorie and I were invited to take part in the Guard of Honour for the Queen, who was to open the kennels. Marjorie was so well behaved as Her Majesty paused to talk to me on her way to the ceremony. She remarked that Marjorie's teeth looked as if they needed some work, and I was so star-struck I didn't know what to say, except 'Yes, Your Majesty.'

After our work with the campaign, there was some exciting news. My sister Imogen was engaged to be married. The wedding would take place at a family friend's home in Scotland where we had enjoyed many family holidays. Marjorie loved running around in the grounds and I knew that, over the wedding weekend, she would be comfortable and familiar with her surroundings. Even more exciting than that was that Imogen wanted Marjorie to be part of the ceremony. 'Oh. my gosh!' I gasped. 'That would be wonderful. Are you sure?'

'Of course! If Marjorie wasn't at my wedding, it would be a tragedy!'

On the day, Marjorie waited patiently until it was our turn to walk down the aisle. She wore a bow tie and waistcoat to match the men in the wedding party. During the ceremony, she was as quiet as a mouse and snuggled beside me when I sat down. Afterwards, she scurried off to her bed and slept through most of the afternoon. But knowing she was nearby, and still a part of the celebration, was lovely for our whole family.

In time, I began taking in foster dogs again, short-term ones so that Marjorie didn't become stressed or agitated. I'd noticed that at times of stress her skin condition would flare up. She was amazing with the dogs I brought home. She could sense when one had had a particularly rough time and left it alone to recuperate. On the other hand, if any wanted to play she would indulge them. As I was studying from home for my child psychology degree, I was on hand to keep an eye on them. I took in just one or two male dogs as I knew Marjorie was uncomfortable around them, no doubt because of her breeding days. She didn't do well with male dogs close to her.

Now Marjorie has settled in and it's clear that her rocky start in life is behind her – though never too far behind. She still suffers skin problems and cysts in her paws, as well as oil in her ears, and will need a lifetime of care. Marjorie will never have the full health she could have enjoyed if she had been taken care of properly from the start, but she has a good quality of life. She is relaxed and playful. Wherever we go, people stop me in the street to talk about her. I am honoured to be her owner and will spend the rest of her life taking care of her and making her happy.

Marjorie is a proud ambassador for Battersea and I'm so glad that I became involved with the charity through the fostering scheme. I joined when it was in its infancy and now it is a huge part of their process. Without the volunteers who help out, things would be very different for Battersea. It's been an amazing experience and I feel proud of what I have achieved with the thirty-nine dogs I have fostered.

With Marjorie in my life – a very happy and contented one – my journey has come full circle.

Our Real-life Teddy Bear

It had been a scorching summer's day, and even though it was now evening, the sky was still bright. All our windows and the back door were open to let in the cooling breeze. As the crescent moon glistened in the sky, there was an impatient knock at the door. A collective groan went up from every corner of our household. Every day for the last week our yellow Labrador, Barney, had been up to mischief and that rapid knock was usually the only warning we had that a neighbour was returning him to us.

This time it was my turn to take the heat so I opened the door, only for Barney to rush past me and into the house, barking his head off. *I'm home! It's me! I'm back! Ha ha ha! You didn't even notice I'd escaped!*

I apologized to our neighbour for Barney's latest fence-jumping and, no doubt, flower-crushing dash through his garden and closed the door, red-faced. Sometimes it seemed Barney was the naughtiest dog in the world. He jumped eight-foot fences, escaped whenever he could into the woods to play with any unsuspecting dogs and owners taking a stroll, rampaged through picnicking families, stealing sausage rolls and sandwiches, stopping only for a quick lick of someone's face, then ran around the green nearby until one of us, or one of our kind neighbours in the little village where we lived, brought him home.

It wasn't as if we hadn't tried. Mum had taken him to obedience classes, tried reinforcing good behaviour and every other trick you can imagine. Dad had replaced our fence three times, each one higher than the last. Eventually our house looked like Fort Knox. There just was no helping Barney. At heart he would be a naughty puppy for ever.

It was the early 1980s and things were very different then from how they are now. It was lucky for my parents, brother, sister and me that we lived in a close-knit and kindly village where everybody knew us and Barney. They say it takes a village to raise a child but in our case it took a village to raise Barney. But for all his mischief everyone loved him. He was often returned to us with a smile, and 'Barney came for a walk with us tonight.' He was the happiest, goofiest dog and made me smile every day. When I was seventeen and began working nearby, I'd get off the bus every evening to find Barney waiting for me on the green opposite the bus stop.

One afternoon, Barney did his usual Houdini trick and disappeared, but that evening, he didn't come back for his dinner. The night dragged on and we began to worry. My mum, who adored Barney, said, 'What if something's happened to him, Sonia?'

'Don't worry, Mum, he'll turn up.'

But Barney didn't turn up, so we began searching everywhere for him. We put posters up asking anyone who found him to call us. We checked with the local police station every day, and spoke to the dog wardens and all the vets in the area. There was no news and yet every day at four forty we refilled his bowl, hoping he'd show up, as he always had done at that time, ready for dinner. Then one or all of us would stand in the garden and shake a box of his favourite biscuits. We were distraught when our boy didn't appear out of the bushes, or from behind the sofa, or come rumbling down the stairs as usual when he heard that box.

Days passed and then Dad received a call. A nurse from the local animal shelter had been out when she'd seen a dog matching Barney's description hit by a car. He'd been taken to Battersea Dogs & Cats Home for emergency treatment as he'd not been wearing a collar. This was before the days of microchipping so we couldn't know if that dog was Barney unless we went to see him. Dad insisted it was best for him to go alone, in case the dog was Barney and he was in a terrible state, but the next day when he was getting ready to leave, I got into the car. 'I'm coming with you, Dad. I don't care what you say.'

He sighed. 'OK, love.'

We arrived and explained our situation and we were told the dog in question had suffered a fracture, but was stable. 'We've set his leg and he should be fine. Would you like to see him?' I prayed that it was Barney because the alternative was too difficult to consider. We were led to the clinic kennels. As we neared them, my dad let out a funny cough. From the end of the row of kennels came a familiar *thump, thump, thump*. My heart soared. I knew we'd get to the kennel in question and Barney would be inside it. Ever since he'd been a puppy, if any of us had made that noise in our throat in the morning while still in bed, Barney's tail would start thumping on the floor: he knew it meant one of us was awake and would soon be coming down to the kitchen where he slept. It was an unmistakable thumping noise, and when we heard it in the kennels, Dad and I looked at each other and smiled.

It was indeed Barney in the kennel and he was as pleased to see us as we were to see him. We were able to have a cuddle and then had a chat with a vet. We explained about Barney's antics and he advised us to have him neutered to calm him down when he had recovered from his accident. We brought Barney home and did as the vet asked and it did help a bit, but not that much. Barney was just a little troublemaker!

We were so grateful to Battersea for taking care of Barney when he'd been in the accident that we gave a donation to the Home every month from then on. I had a special place in my heart for it, and the dedication with which they'd taken care of Barney was truly inspiring.

When I was twenty-three, I moved to my own home with my partner, around the corner from my parents. I was training as a dental nurse when I found out I was pregnant. It was a surprise, and as the months passed and my belly grew, I daydreamed about the family life we would have. I had always wanted a dog of my own and wondered when the time would be right to find one.

Our daughter, Annie, was just a month old when my brother Stuart called, sounding very distressed. 'It's Barney,' he said. 'We've had to put him to sleep.'

I could hardly believe what I'd heard. 'What? What happened?'

Stuart explained that old age had caught up with Barney and, very suddenly, his organs had failed. The vet had had to put him to sleep. It was very upsetting for us all, and Mum couldn't talk to me or anyone else.

I took the news hard and found myself crying a lot. It was difficult to accept that our adorable, mischievous Barney was gone. But gradually I started to come to terms with our loss. Barney had lived to the ripe old age of seventeen. He'd had a wonderful life, full of fun and adventure, and had been loved by everyone who had known him.

Mum particularly struggled with losing him. He'd very much been her dog. 'I'll never have another dog,' she told me. 'I can't go through this pain again. Once in a lifetime is enough for me.'

I hoped she would change her mind, but she never did. Instead, she walked many of the dogs in the village and was the first person her friends thought of if they needed someone to look after their dog while they were away.

But I still dreamt of having my own dog. I wanted Annie to experience what I had as a child, the enduring friendship of a dog. He or she didn't fall out with you, stop loving you, go off with a new best friend or get bored with you. That unconditional love was priceless. But Annie's father was a cat person and I was allergic to cats. The dog versus cat debate was one that we revisited over the many years of our relationship.

When our son, Jack, arrived, his father and I discussed once more the possibility of having a dog or a cat, but it was only when our relationship had ended, and I was raising the kids on my own, that I let myself consider getting a dog.

Like me, Jack loved dogs and Annie, like her dad, preferred cats. I was already putting all my energy into raising the children and didn't feel I had it in me to be responsible for a dog too. Also, I was worried that Jack's asthma, which he had inherited from me, might be exacerbated by a pet. Once again, the idea went on the back-burner.

In time, I met my new partner, Simon, who moved in with me and the kids. Our family life was full but that didn't stop the children asking for a pet. They made the same arguments I'm sure every other reluctant parent has heard. 'We'll walk it! We'll take care of it! We promise! Please!'

Then something happened to take the decision out of our hands. One evening, my sister, Tina, called: 'Sonia, you have to come over. My lodger has found two puppies and you need to see them.'

'No, I can't. If I see them, I'll want them and then I'll be in trouble!'

'Just come round – please!'

One was a Jack Russell Pug cross and the other a Bichon Frise. But they were very small and had clearly escaped from someone's home near to where the lodger had found them. She'd knocked on the doors around there but hadn't been able to trace the owner. She had already alerted the police, RSPCA and local vets.

'Just come round and see them tonight while I still have them,' Tina wheedled.

I thought about it – and decided to take the kids too. We pushed back Simon's birthday-dinner plans so that we could visit the puppies, and they were adorable. We played with them, held them and stroked them, and a part of me I had buried deep seemed to come alive. I wanted to scoop them both into my arms and run all the way home with them. 'Well, why don't you keep one, Sonia?' the lodger said.

'That's not how it works, unfortunately,' I said. 'Some poor soul is missing these two puppies. We have to try to find the owner, and return the puppies to him or her.'

The kids were besotted with them and so was I but we left to go and have dinner. Our conversation was entirely about the puppies. I couldn't concentrate on anything else.

Next day, Tina said she couldn't keep the puppies at her home for much longer so I took them home with me. I'd care for them until we could track down the local authority's dog warden. For some reason, my local authority didn't have one, so I called the neighbouring borough's and reported the dogs missing. I made a poster and stuck it up in the supermarket and other shops near where the puppies had been found. I didn't say what breeds they were because I wanted to make sure their true owner came forward.

I started receiving calls. One person claimed to have lost a brindle dog, which didn't fit, and others, who had no idea what breed the dogs were, lied to me because they wanted to see the puppies. It was quite disturbing how many people called without having any connection to the dogs.

The Enfield dog warden was happy for me to continue taking care of the pups until there was a development. After two weeks, the owner contacted me. As so much time had passed, I was in two minds about keeping the puppies, but when the man explained what had happened, I knew it was only right to return them. Apparently the puppies had been playing outside when somehow they had slipped out of the gates and onto the main road where my sister's lodger had found them.

He explained how distressed his two children were and how much they were missing the puppies. His description of them was spot on, and after guidance from the dog warden, I prepared to say goodbye to the puppies. I bathed them both and the four of us drove over to drop them off.

Afterwards, I cried for weeks. I missed their little faces, the little noises they made, and suddenly our home seemed devoid of life. I realized, too, that in the weeks the pups had been with us, both my asthma and Jack's had been fine. Neither of us had reacted. It had proved a trial run and I felt ready, after so many years, to take the leap and get our own dog.

Simon agreed. 'It'll be really good for the kids,' he said.

Without telling the children, Simon and I began searching for a rescue dog to take in. But we couldn't find one that was the right fit for our family. Jack was nine and Annie was fourteen. We were hoping for a young, healthy dog as I wanted the kids to have the experience I'd had growing up with Barney. We wanted a dog that would be a long-term fixture in our family and could grow up with the kids.

After a few weeks of searching without success, I turned my attention to Battersea Dogs & Cats Home. I'd avoided it until then as it was quite a distance away from our home in Hertfordshire but now I couldn't wait any longer for a dog.

I called Battersea and we were told to come along for an interview, bringing everyone in our household, so Simon, Annie, Jack and I drove over that weekend. The kids were so excited.

When we'd completed our interview, the rehomer said, 'I have a match for you. His name is Teddy and he's a Staffordshire Bull Terrier.'

Teddy had been taken to Battersea by his previous family. They had loved him very much but their young daughter wasn't well and they could no longer care for him. It had been a sad decision for the family, but the right one. We were taken to a room to meet him, and when the door opened, he rushed in and raced around. Instantly, we were all smiling. Teddy was interested in everyone and everything, and very excited to meet us. 'He's very lively, isn't he?' I said.

I worried that perhaps Teddy was *too* lively, but as we played with him he calmed down a little. He was very keen on Jack and wouldn't leave him alone.

'It's a good sign that Teddy has picked the youngest in your family as his first friend,' the rehomer told us.

We took him for a walk and I noticed Teddy was strong and quite muscly. He was in good shape and, clearly, his previous owners had taken proper care of his nutrition and exercise. Jack took the lead and, to my surprise, Teddy didn't pull on it. He was very happy and bouncy and had us all laughing.

Jack's face was lit up and so was Annie's.

'What do you think, kids?'

'Can we take him? Please, Mum?' said Jack.

'Can we?' Annie chimed in.

We continued our walk, and Simon and I talked quietly while the kids went ahead of us with Teddy. When we'd gone to Battersea, we'd had no idea what type of dog we were after but we knew we wanted a medium to large one that was great with the kids and happy. Teddy ticked all the boxes. 'I think Teddy's perfect,' Simon said.

I still wanted to be sure we were making the right decision. Ultimately, the kids would be at school and Simon would be at work, so Teddy would largely be my responsibility. We took a seat on the bench near the paddocks and I pictured Teddy snoozing by our fireplace on a winter evening. Then I imagined being out and about with him. At that moment, a couple walked past. 'He's lovely,' the woman said. 'Are you taking him?'

Before anyone else could answer, I said, 'Yes! Yes, we are.' There was no way I could let Teddy go.

The kids were delighted and I asked the rehomer if we could return the following day to collect Teddy. She agreed and we completed the paperwork. As we lived more than an hour away, we could have taken Teddy that day but I wanted a little time to think it over to be doubly sure that it was the right decision.

I tossed and turned all night and worried myself into a headache. I knew I was overthinking it, and the next day we drove back to Battersea to pick Teddy up. We took our seats in Reception and I wondered if he would recognize us when he came out.

Dog after dog trotted past us without much fuss and then, suddenly, a brindle-coloured Staffie appeared, his tail and bum wiggling furiously. He pulled his handler towards us and gave us lots of licks. 'So you do remember us, Teddy, don't you?' He looked up at me with his gorgeous brown eyes and let out a double woof. *Of course I remember you!*

On the journey home, I looked in the back and saw that Jack had fallen asleep with Teddy across his lap. It was a beautiful moment in our family life, a snippet of the future and happy times to come.

Teddy settled into our home very quickly and I noticed he slept a lot. I figured the last few weeks had been so tiring for him that he needed to catch up, but after a while, we all came to see that Teddy was a really old soul and liked to laze around! He was mostly calm but when one of us came into the room, he'd jump up and greet us.

Everyone who met Teddy said what a gentle and lovely dog he was and even Mum and Dad, who had been a bit worried about us getting a Staffie, came to see that their anxiety about the breed was entirely misplaced.

The night before we brought Teddy home, I'd called Mum to tell her our news. 'Oh, Sonia. Why don't you get a nice Labrador instead?' Now Mum was as mad about Teddy as we were. She had even taken to stopping and greeting any Staffie she saw on the street. I wished more people knew what a lovely breed they are, and sometimes I set people straight when they misjudged Teddy.

Once I was out with Teddy when a man came past with his Bichon Frise. He stopped as we neared to let us pass. 'It's OK, thanks,' I said. 'You carry on.'

'I'm not walking past your dog,' he said.

'It's all right, honestly. Teddy's really friendly.'

But the man wouldn't listen. 'They're not friendly.'

I was becoming quite upset now. 'They are lovely dogs, really.'

Meanwhile, his little dog was barking and barking at Teddy while Teddy gazed at me silently: *Please make it go away. Why is it so noisy?*

I wanted to educate the man a bit but he was too stubborn to listen.

Time passed, and Annie had taken Teddy for a walk one evening when my mobile began to ring. I answered, it was Annie in tears. Teddy had been attacked. 'Mum, help!' I rushed in my car to find them. I spotted Annie beside the road not far from our house, and she piled in with Teddy in her arms. She was crying hysterically and Teddy was shaking and whining.

Apparently, Teddy and Annie had been looking at the horses in the field near our home when a German Shepherd had come flying out of nowhere and clamped its jaws around Teddy's neck. Teddy hadn't barked or growled or shown any reaction, he'd simply lain down on the pavement and started to houl. 'He was shaking, Mum. He was so scared. I've never heard cries like that from him. It was awful.'

I felt so angry and upset. And to think that dogs like Teddy had an undeserved reputation, thanks in part to the media. He hadn't even fought back. I checked him over and found puncture wounds on the back of his neck where the other dog had broken the skin. We took him to the vet, who prescribed antibiotics, and when we returned home, we called the police. We knew which house the dog had come from so they took a statement from us, then went to talk to the other party.

In the end, nothing came of it but we knew to avoid that route from now on. I wasn't going to take any risks with Annie or Teddy.

Weeks later, we took Teddy to our local dog competition and entered him in the Best Rescue Dog category. We were thrilled when he was placed first because he thoroughly deserved it: he was a best friend to all of us and was everything you could hope for in a family dog. I was so glad he was ours.

Not long after that, Jack became unwell and Teddy's friendship and love became even more important. Jack was suffering with alopecia and lost his hair, eyebrows and eyelashes. It was a very difficult time for him as he was only twelve and the children at his school didn't understand. He had a terrible time, and some days he came home too upset to speak. Teddy was always there. He sat with Jack, lay down beside him, spent time with him. They played together when Jack was up to it, and when he wasn't Teddy climbed up on the sofa and rested his chin on my son's leg as if to say, *I'm here, mate.*

I'd learnt from spending so much time with Teddy that he was exceptionally intuitive and he could tell when Jack needed space or comfort. Whichever it was, Teddy just knew what to do. In the end, Jack had to have a year off school as the medication for the condition made him poorly. Teddy helped us all through it, and I was happy to know that at any given point in the day, Teddy was available for cuddles with Jack. I found, too, that Teddy had a way of soothing Jack when nobody else could. He brought us all a lot of comfort at a difficult time for our family.

I took him for walks three times a day and that routine, fresh air and time away from the house, gave me a chance to regroup and get myself together on hard days. When I saw a competition on Twitter from Battersea to find man's best friend and meet the Queen, I didn't hesitate in entering Teddy. I posted a picture of him on my lap in a beer garden with the caption: *Teddy thinks he is royalty and we do too. Make a Staffie smile.*

A week passed and I scanned all the other pictures entered in the competition. There were so many – did we stand a chance? Another week went by, and I got a phone call to say Teddy had been shortlisted. We couldn't believe it! They asked me for some more information so I sent it by email and was told somebody would be in touch. I tried not to get my hopes up but as the competition narrowed to just me and one other potential winner, I had butterflies in my belly. The final stage was for Kate, a member of the Battersea team, to come to my home and meet Teddy. She came over, took Teddy for a walk and spent some time with him. After she'd left, I told Simon, 'I reckon we're in with a good chance.'

'I'm sure Teddy did his best!'

Next day, I was on tenterhooks. When my phone rang it was Kate. 'Sonia, I wanted to let you know the outcome of the competition to meet the Queen.'

'Yes,' I said. 'And?'

'We'd like you and Teddy to present a gift to the Queen at the opening of our new kennels.'

I must have whooped because Kate began laughing.

I squeezed Teddy. 'We did it!

Teddy understood something exciting was happening because his tail was going like the clappers. That Monday, I took him to Battersea and spent a day meeting the people who work there to rehearse for the opening of the new kennels. I was given a pack of information, including the timings for the big day and the dress code. Teddy and I were announced as the competition winners and the messages poured in on Twitter. I had tweets from Buckingham Palace, and complete strangers complimented me on how lovely Teddy was. It was overwhelming, flattering and so exciting.

I wasn't able to take anyone with me, but on the day Teddy and I got ready and a car came to collect us. While everyone was queuing outside to get a glimpse of the Queen as she arrived, I was ushered straight through. I felt like a VIP as I bypassed some of Battersea's biggest supporters. They all looked at me curiously. *Who is she?*

I was shown to the marquee and a seat with my name on it. The model David Gandy was just a few feet away from me, as well as a lot of other famous supporters of the Home. I recognized some of the vets from *Paul O'Grady: For the Love of Dogs*.

Strangest of all, people I didn't know were aware of who I was. I felt like a star and so did Teddy. He jumped up on my lap to get a better look at everyone. I don't think Teddy had ever received so many treats in one night.

Then it was time for the Queen to unveil the plaque, which read: *To commemorate the opening of the Mary Tealby Kennels by Her Majesty the Queen, 17 March 2015.* Around the edge, the plaque read: *Battersea Dogs & Cats Home, where life begins again.* I watched with pride from the side of the stage as the Queen completed her duties. Then a voice came over the microphone. It was Claire Horton, chief executive of Battersea Dogs & Cats

Home: 'And now we have Sonia Robertson here with Teddy to present a gift.'

I stepped forward to a round of applause and gave Her Majesty a bag of goodies for her own dogs. She gave me the biggest smile. 'Thank you.'

Part of the pack I'd been given days earlier provided information on royal protocol, such as not speaking to the Queen unless she spoke to you first, not touching her and so on. Later in the line-up, Teddy sat perfectly as the Queen walked past us all. She said hello, so I curtsied and said, 'Your Majesty.'

At the end of the night, a taxi took us home. What an exhilarating evening it had been. When I got into the house I told the family about every second of the day and they all beamed with pride. Teddy was too tired to listen so he slumped against me on the sofa and slept soundly as I recounted the best bits. After the kids had gone to bed, I stayed up late watching videos of the evening on YouTube.

After that, whenever anyone in the family said they'd done something exciting, I always responded, 'But have you met the Queen?'

Battersea is so special to me. My journey with the Home began with Barney decades ago and eventually brought Teddy to me. Whenever I'm there, I feel at home and I know Teddy feels the same.

Battersea will always be close to our hearts.

Minty

They say you are either a cat person or a dog person. Well, I had always considered myself a dog person through and through. I'd grown up in a small village in the Worcestershire countryside, and when I was thirteen, we'd taken in a puppy from a working farm nearby. His mum and dad were Border Collies and Sam had inherited their intelligence. He was bouncy, full of beans, loved to run and was supersmart. He could catch a Frisbee or a tennis ball and Mum worked hard to get him to sit, stay, roll over and come to heel with puppy training classes. But until his dying day, aged twelve, Sam hated being on a lead. However, he made up for that with so many other things.

Sam could read how every person in our house was feeling at any particular moment. Whenever my brother, Adam, and I were packing our bags to go back to university, Sam lost his bounce. He sat curled up on his bed, aware that the atmosphere had changed with us about to leave home again. He was a huge part of our family and we all loved him dearly.

So, some years on, when my husband, Ben, and I talked about getting a pet, our opinions were split. I wanted a dog but Ben wanted a cat. 'It's all moot anyway until we buy our own place, Emily,' Ben would say.

We were living in a little rented house in Oxfordshire, and, over time, a neighbourhood cat started coming to visit. She popped in and out of our garden and I became quite fond of her. We didn't know her name but she was white so we called her Snowy. In the summer, she'd sneak into our house looking for cuddles and a tasty bite and we grew quite used to anticipating her next appearance.

She was so full of character that I started to see why Ben wanted a cat so much. With both of us out at work for twelve hours a day, a dog really wasn't a feasible option. And that was when I began to realize that maybe I wasn't just a dog person after all.

When we moved to London for work, we lived in flats for eight years and daydreamed about getting a rescue cat when we had a garden of our own. The idea of a kitten was lovely but we'd seen friends with kittens and knew how much time had to go into caring for them. With our working hours, it wasn't going to be possible. Plus, Ben and I wanted to start a family one day: We liked the idea of getting an adult cat from Battersea Dogs & Cats Home, where the animals are profiled and you get some idea of a cat's temperament.

When we were able to put in an offer on a semi-detached house in Surrey, we were just one step away from making our cat dream a reality. The sale took six months and we became friends with the lady who was selling the house to us, Suzy. After we exchanged, she called with an unusual request. 'My new house is going to take a little longer than I expected to be ready, so I'm having to move into temporary accommodation for a fortnight. Trouble is, they won't let me bring my cat. How would you feel about looking after Tash for those two weeks?'

'Let me speak to Ben and I'll call you back.'

Ben thought it was an unusual request too, but in a way it made sense. Rather than putting Tash into a cattery, he would stay in the house he was used to and we'd get a test run at looking after him full time. 'Let's do it.'

I let Suzy know and she was delighted. 'He's very self-contained and goes in and out all the time. You won't really see him, except at mealtimes and when he's ready for a good sleep.'

When we moved our furniture in, Suzy was there to hand over Tash and his things. She was grateful for our help and we were happy to do her the favour because we were doing ourselves one at the same time. Our new house was much bigger than we were used to and having another being roaming around made it feel more like home.

We'd never looked after a cat before but Tash was a dream. He was as independent as Suzy had described, but in the evenings, he liked to curl up on the couch with us. And it wasn't unusual to wake up in the middle of the night and find a nice warm cat lying on our feet. Tash was thirteen, and very relaxed. He was a joy to have around. When Suzy picked him up, the house felt awfully empty. Tash had made our house a home before we'd even finished unpacking. Now I felt bereft.

Ben and I had bought the house with a five-year renovation plan in mind. 'I know we wanted to wait two years before we got a cat so that some of the work would be done, but I don't think I can wait that long,' I said.

Ben nodded. 'I know what you mean. It seems so far away.'

As my birthday loomed closer, Ben planned a nice lunch in town to cheer me up. It was Sunday, but both of us dressed up and caught the train into town. We got off the tube in Vauxhall and began the short walk to the restaurant. As the famous chimneys of Battersea Power Station loomed into view, my stomach did a flip. I squeezed Ben's hand. 'Where are you taking me?'

He smiled. 'We're going to lunch, but first we have an appointment with Battersea to talk about rehoming a cat.'

It was the best possible birthday surprise, and even though I was wearing heels, I practically ran to the gates of the Home. We were let in by security and went through to the main reception. I was so excited I could hardly contain myself. We were taken to a room for an interview, and as we sat down, I felt a pang of nerves. What if we were deemed unsuitable for a cat? What would we do then?

I needn't have worried. After we'd had a good chat, the rehomer said, 'You're excellent candidates. Shall we take a look around the cattery?'

As we walked towards it, I explained that I was hoping for a female cat. I'd read online that males were more prone to straying and less affectionate. There were a number of female cats ready for rehoming but we were not the right match. As first-time owners, the cats with medical needs weren't the right fit for us.

Our options were dwindling, and then the rehomer said, 'Would you consider taking in a pair? We have a number of brother and sister duos, but we can't split them up.'

Ben was open to it, but I was worried that, as a first pet, two would prove too much.

'Come on, Emily,' Ben said. 'At least let's meet some of the boys.'

'OK,' I said.

We were shown to a pen containing a two-year-old cat named Mentos. It looked empty but the rehomer explained Mentos was a stray who'd survived on the streets for a year before he was picked up. While he'd been fending for himself, his skin had become irritated and he had pulled out all of his fur. 'It's grown back now, bar a few patches on his tail, but he's quite shy, hence the sheet we've put up for him to hide behind.' As I was looking at the street a little face poked out. Mentos had eyes as big as saucers and he was gorgeous.

'Can I meet him?'

The rehomer nodded. 'It might help if you were to go down on all fours and try to give him a treat.'

I felt silly but I did as she said and Mentos eventually came out. His dark eyes were wide with anxiety but he crept forward when I offered him a little orange fish toy made of felt. Battersea supporters make toys for the cats and Mentos loved his. As I sat with him, he began to play with me and I thought how sweet he was. After a while, Ben and I swapped places. When Ben came out, we shut the door of the pen. Mentos jumped onto his box and hung his head. He looked so forlorn as we walked away that I felt a rush of love for him. He must have thought we were leaving him for good. I snapped a picture of him to look at over lunch.

'We don't know much about his background,' the rehomer told us, 'but we think Mentos will be great with kids. And, given that he was a stray for so long, he'll be fine on his own while you're both at work.'

Ben and I decided to reserve him and headed off for lunch. We talked it over and decided we definitely wanted Mentos. How could we leave him when he so desperately needed a loving home?

Over lunch, we talked nonstop about our new family member, and afterwards, we called Battersea to let them know we'd pick him up the next day. Then we went shopping for a cat bed, food and water bowls, and a litter tray. I was all dolled up from my birthday lunch and must have looked ridiculously out of place, but I didn't care because we had a cat! We lugged it all home on the bus, and set up Mentos's things in the kitchen.

The next morning, we returned by train to collect him. As we finished off the paperwork, we jotted down Mentos's new name: Minty. It was linked to his Battersea name but seemed to us to suit him. I'd been concerned that changing his name would confuse him but the staff at Battersea had reassured us that he'd be fine with it. All the while, Minty was sitting calmly in a cat carrier on the table next to us. He was making little squeaks and seemed as happy as we were.

He miaowed all the way home on the bus, and when we finally arrived, we placed his carrier on the floor in the hallway and opened the door. We'd been told to keep him indoors for a week or two as he was likely to be overwhelmed by all the upheaval but nothing could have prepared us for the next few hours. When Minty came out of the cage, he wriggled out flat on his belly. He slithered around like that for a few minutes. We watched him for a while. 'I think something's wrong with his back,' Ben said. 'I'm really concerned.'

I was too. Minty could barely walk and seemed very much in distress. We followed him from room to room and he kept glancing at us. He got halfway up the stairs, slumped on the corner step with his back to the wall and closed his eyes. He looked exhausted. 'If he's still like this in an hour, let's call the vets at Battersea,' Ben said.

I nodded.

But half an hour later, Minty got up and made his way to the kitchen. We'd put his cosy basket in there, and it had a hood on it to give him somewhere to hide. As soon as he spotted it, he straightened up and darted inside it. We realized he had just been scared. The noise of the journey home, being in a cat carrier and now a strange house with no familiar smells had spooked him.

After a few minutes we smelt something unpleasant. Minty had pooed in his basket. We cleaned it out and showed him where the litter tray was. We hadn't put it in clear view and the stress of the day had got the better of him. Over the next couple of hours, Minty took some treats, used the litter tray and appeared much better. Next morning, he was waiting for us in the kitchen and followed me around the house. I had taken the day off work and Ben was at home the following day so that we both spent some time with Minty. We didn't want to leave him alone so soon.

In the evening, Minty slept on the sofa next to us. I was relieved that he was settling in and being himself. He struggled with wearing a collar and kept trying to get it off. I knew it must be uncomfortable as he wasn't used to wearing one, but it was for the best. We were very pleased that he was becoming playful, which meant he was coming out of his shell. The glimpse of personality he had shown us at the

Home was now shining through. His favourite toy was still the little knitted orange fish we'd brought with him from Battersea and he liked to drop it in the kitchen, then bounce back a minute later to pick it up and run upstairs with it. He was very lively and happy and we smiled to see him pottering around our home.

As the long Easter weekend loomed, we decided it would be a good time to let Minty out for the first time. A cat flap had been installed in the kitchen, one of those which read a microchip and allowed only Minty to come inside. It would be great to stop other adventurous cats, like Snowy, creeping in! Setting that weekend for his first outing had a number of bonuses: Ben's grandmother would be staying with us and she had years of experience with cats, and it gave me time to get to grips with the idea of letting him out. I was very nervous that he would get a renewed taste for the outdoors and never return!

Minty's big day arrived, and when I woke up, I felt a swishing above my head, then something soft and warm tickling my nose. I opened my eyes to find Minty's face peering down at me from the headboard. He'd taken to sitting up there in the morning, miaowing loudly until one of us relented and got up to feed him. He'd already shown himself to be a greedy little cat! Our vet had assured us we were feeding him the right amount, with his two square meals a day, but

Minty was a little food monster: anything left on the worktops and, *whoosh!*, it was gone in seconds. He'd lick coleslaw out of the pot and swipe food from your hand if you weren't careful.

Now, as Minty stared at me, flicking his tail back and forth between my head and Ben's, I smiled. 'Come on, then, little one. Let's get you some brekkie.' I got out of bed and Minty chirruped in the particular way he did when he jumped down from somewhere. He wove in and out of my legs as I went to the bathroom and pulled my dressing-gown on. He danced down the stairs and shot into the kitchen to stare at his bowl. *Come on, then*, he miaowed.

I gave him his breakfast, and then we sat down, with Ben's gran, to have ours.

'Let's get that cat outside,' Ben said, when we'd finished.

I groaned. 'I'm so nervous.'

But Ben and his gran were reassuring. 'We'll all keep an eye on him. He's not going to get lost, I promise,' Ben said.

We unlocked the cat flap and stepped outside to encourage Minty to follow us. We shut the door behind us and flapped the cat flap a few times, calling Minty. Every time we looked inside, he was peering at us through the flap. I was sure he was telling us, *Nope. Not doing it. I'm not coming through that thing*. It looked like my worries about Minty running off were quite unfounded.

After an hour, we were all perplexed. 'He's not getting this, is he?' said Ben.

'I have an idea,' I said. I ducked inside the kitchen where Minty was flat on his back. I grabbed his treats box, and as soon as he heard the rattle of the biscuits, his ears spun around and he propped himself up. He looked very pleased with himself: he was about to get a treat for nothing. Instead of giving him one, though, I stepped outside into the garden and shut the door. Minty was very food-driven: if anything was going to get him through that flap, it was the biscuits in my hand.

I rattled them again and poked my hand through the cat flap. After a few shakes, Minty's paw punched the little door. I kept shaking the box until his head poked through. '*Voilà!*' I said, as Minty tumbled out onto the patio. He looked a little shell-shocked at first, but once he was on his feet and trotting around, he was very much at ease.

We kept the cat flap open with a bit of string for a few hours: we'd realized that the click of the lock when it read Minty's microchip was freaking him out. In the meantime, he padded around the garden where Ben had scattered some of his litter at the edges. We'd been told it would make him feel settled, like a scent mark, and we walked with him as he began to explore. Suddenly he leapt up the eight-foot fence and disappeared into our neighbour's garden.

'Minty!' we both shouted.

I was terrified that we'd lost him, but Gran just chuckled. 'Don't worry, he'll come back.'

I paced the lawn for ten minutes until we heard a scrabbling at the spot where he'd disappeared. It was surely Minty but, for whatever reason, he couldn't get back up the fence to us. Ben went round and fetched him from the neighbour. It turned out the lawn on the other side was a foot lower than ours, so the fence was too high for him.

We went back inside. 'That's enough for one day,' I said.

Next day, we tried again, and this time Minty ventured out much more easily and my worry subsided. Time and time again, Minty went out and returned home to sleep in his own bed. Whatever freedom he enjoyed when he was out and about, it was clear that his home comforts surpassed it.

When our home renovations got under way, Minty turned out to be untroubled by the noise and upheaval. He hung around the builders, and despite the banging and the dust, he loved being in the thick of it. When our floorboards were being ripped up for work underneath, Minty's head would pop up in the gaps and he loved lurking about under our house, exploring the space. I reckoned his hardiness from his time on the streets was reasserting itself.

Given what he'd been through as a stray, we were continually surprised by how friendly and trusting Minty was. He loved to sit on anyone's lap, and at

Christmas, when almost everyone was vying to have cuddles with him, he managed to pick the one person who wasn't that interested in him: my father-in-law, Phillip. Minty didn't care that Dad wasn't keen. He pummelled him with his paws, miaowed for attention and purred his head off. It really made us laugh and, soon enough, Dad softened.

It was a fun time for Minty, too, in terms of food. There was so much of it knocking around, and although we'd warned everyone not to feed him scraps because he would always beg for more, Minty found some exciting ways to get in on the action. One evening, Mum was eating a mince pie when Minty pounced and grabbed it out of her hand. He ran away with it and ate it in his basket. Another day, he jumped on Ben and snatched a ham sandwich off his plate. Ben gave chase but Minty darted through the cat flap with it and sat in the middle of the lawn to eat his plunder! He set a whole new precedent, though, when he knocked a lunchbox with gammon inside it off the kitchen counter and onto the floor. Of course, the lid flew off, and when we went in to see what was going on, Minty had the gammon in his paws and was chomping away at it!

The vet had told us that the stray in him would continue to scavenge for food so we did our best to keep him away from anything that would harm him, but he often managed to outwit us.

When Minty wasn't swiping food or stashing a treat in his basket for later, he liked to doze by the fire until he was so hot that it felt like his fur was on fire. Other times, we'd find him snoozing under our duvet. By the following winter he had become the centre of our universe and we rarely went out or left him alone when we were not at work. But one such evening, we set his dinner timer for six o'clock and headed for a curry after work. We returned home at nine. Ben went in ahead of me and stopped abruptly. Usually Minty was waiting for us when he heard the key in the lock, and I thought Ben had paused so that he didn't tread on him. Then he said, 'Emily, stay right there.'

'Why?' I said. 'What is it?'

Before Ben answered, we both heard it. Minty was crying somewhere. As Ben rushed upstairs, I gasped. There was a trail of blood on our beige carpet.

As Ben rounded the corner onto our upstairs landing, I heard him gasp. 'Oh, God, Minty . . .'

By now my heart was in my throat. I raced upstairs after him, and when I saw Minty, my eyes stung with tears. He had injured his back leg very badly: it was mangled and there was blood everywhere. He'd obviously been all around the house looking for us before curling up underneath the desk in the study next to the radiator. I bent down and saw that his usually pink nose was as white as chalk. He'd obviously lost a lot of blood and was in shock.

A wave of guilt washed through me. While we'd been having our curry, Minty had been in desperate need of our help. We called an emergency vet as it was now after nine on a Friday night and were told to wrap Minty in a blanket and bring him into the surgery. He squealed and tried to run away from us when we attempted to pick him up, clearly in a lot of pain, but eventually I managed to wrap him up and put him in his cat carrier. We drove to the emergency clinic and Minty was very distressed in the car. He hated being in it on the best of days but now he was crying and mewing nonstop.

As soon as we got through the door, the vet and the on-call nurse whipped Minty away to examine him. Ben and I were left pacing the empty waiting room. After fifteen minutes, the vet returned. 'I think he's been hit by a car. We've sedated him and put him on a drip. He's too traumatized right now to let us do a scan or an X-ray so the next twelve hours are critical.' She added, 'From my initial examination, I think we'll have to amputate his damaged leg.' I began to cry and Ben put his arm around me.

There was nothing more we could do so we returned home. I didn't sleep a wink that night, thinking about poor Minty. He'd survived a year on the streets unscathed but now look at him! Did the damage mean we'd have to put him down? He couldn't live on three legs, could he?

Next morning I lay in bed and sobbed.

After a while, Ben said, 'Come on. We've got to be strong for Minty. They haven't rung us yet so he's obviously survived the night. Come into the garden and help me until they call.'

I did as Ben suggested and pottered about distractedly, unable to get anything done.

At two o'clock, they called. We learnt that not only did Minty's back leg need to be amputated, but his right hip was dislocated. It was bad news but at least his internal organs appeared to be unscathed. However, if Minty survived his injuries and the surgery, he would need an eight-week rehabilitation programme.

That afternoon, we went to see him and he was out of it, his eyes glazed, because of the pain medication. We gave him a kiss and returned home. On Sunday, we went back to see him and this time he was much brighter. His mangled leg was in plaster to stop it moving around until the amputation on Monday. He responded to us and looked glad to see us. It felt so good to have our boy back, and with his leg bandaged, he seemed almost fine. But we knew that wasn't so and that a long road to recovery lay ahead of him.

The following day, Minty's operation was a success and we were able to bring him home. He was wearing a special collar to stop him pulling out his stitches and had to be kept in a large recovery cage. It would stop him moving around over the next eight weeks, and certainly didn't allow him enough room to try to jump.

The first few days went quite well. Minty was still on painkillers and antibiotics so he slept quite a lot. But as he became more aware of his surroundings, he kept trying to move in his cage and the collar meant he often got his head stuck. He also found it hard to use the litter tray, as balancing in there on three legs was difficult. It was distressing for him as well as heart-breaking for us.

As he worked harder and harder to reach his stitches, we decided to carry the cage upstairs to our room each night. We knew we wouldn't sleep for worrying about him alone and miserable downstairs. For eight weeks, we woke in the middle of the night to sort Minty out. He was becoming increasingly angry that he was being kept in a cage, and whenever we changed his litter or put his food in, he tried to escape. He was showing so much spirit and had so much fight in him: all of that told me he would be OK for sure.

In the end, his reluctant confinement and our hard work paid off: his right hip recovered well from the dislocation. The amputation was difficult to adjust to, however. Minty had phantom-limb syndrome, according to the vet, because he could feel it was still there. He tried to scratch his left ear with his stump and fell over when he tried to put weight on the missing leg.

When we had to return to work, our mums each took a week off to come over to our house and take care of him. They were brilliant.

My mum even brought with her a book called *Little Kitten's First Christmas*. It was the story of an adult cat reading to a little kitten. Every time she read it to Minty, he would fall asleep. We also discovered that he felt the cold a lot more than he had before his accident, as he wasn't able to move around normally, so twice a day we gave him a hot-water bottle. He liked to prop himself up on it, using the bottle in place of his missing leg. All in all, he coped well and had soon adjusted to balancing on three legs. It meant that he moved in a diagonal motion but, other than that, he could get around without problems.

Three months after his accident, we let him outside again. We were both very nervous about there being another accident but we couldn't keep him inside for ever. He had conquered the cat flap within a few hours and was soon running around at startling speed. He was such a survivor and I felt very proud of him.

By the summer, when his fur had grown back, people came to visit and didn't notice for hours that our cat had only three legs. I learnt there was a whole community of resilient tripod cats and I was proud to know that our Minty was part of it.

One night, Ben went out with his friends. When he called to check on us at nine o'clock, I realized Minty had been out for a few hours without returning. I went outside, called for him and shook his treats. He didn't return. The time ticked by to ten o'clock, then eleven, then midnight. Minty had still not returned. Ben and I went to bed but I was filled with dread. I was awake all night and Ben woke up multiple times. Every time he did, he asked, 'Is he back yet?'

By seven the next morning, I was almost delirious with worry. It was as if the six months since the accident had disappeared, and we were back to the moment when we'd discovered Minty covered with blood in the study. I was beside myself as I stood in the garden, scanning the fences, hoping to see the familiar black-and-white blur.

I returned to the kitchen a sobbing mess. Then, suddenly, the cat flap went. 'Ben, he's here!' I shouted.

Minty was covered with grey dust, and we reckoned he'd been trapped in a barbecue overnight or on a building site, maybe even in someone's dusty old shed. Wherever he had been, I no longer cared, because he was home! I gave him breakfast and he was so hungry that he gobbled it down in seconds. It took an extra bowl of food before he trotted away.

As Minty got older he ventured out less. I was grateful to have him around and within sight. I couldn't help but worry when he was out. One evening, as he snuggled under the duvet with us, it made me think back to that day at Battersea. I had been adamant that I wanted a girl cat because it would be more affectionate and less likely to stray. How wrong I had been! Minty was as soft as anything and craved human contact at any moment of the day. He was perfect.

In time, Ben and I planned to start a family and we looked into how we could go about bringing a baby into our home without Minty feeling sidelined. Our friends knew how much we spoilt Minty, and when we told them we were expecting, they joked that Minty would no longer be the apple of our eye. 'He'll be forgotten when that baby comes home with you,' they said.

But Ben and I were adamant that wouldn't happen. 'He's our firstborn,' we said – and, really, he was like our first baby. We reasoned that if Minty got jealous of the baby once it arrived, we'd have nobody to blame but ourselves. We vowed to make sure he got his fair share of attention and care.

Two months before the baby was due, we stopped Minty sleeping on our bed in an effort to get him used to his basket in the kitchen, where he had slept happily before his accident. I wondered if it would be difficult to transfer him from one to the other, because if we shut him into another room in daytime – if I had a delivery and had to open the front door – he would howl. To my surprise, he coped fine with being in the kitchen again at night. There wasn't a peep out of him. I hoped that would be a sign of good things to follow.

In February 2015, I gave birth to a healthy baby boy, Arthur. He'd arrived three weeks early so we were both kept in hospital for a week, while Ben rushed around like mad getting the house ready for the baby. We hadn't been expecting him so soon so Ben had to buy the final things we needed and finish setting up the nursery.

The day we were due to come home, Ben said, 'I hope Minty copes OK. I haven't really been around to give him any attention and he noticed you were missing. And now we'll be returning with a very noisy little extra person!'

'I'm sure he'll be OK. We've prepared for this.'

I'd done a lot of reading on the Internet about how best to introduce a cat to a baby. When we got into the house, Minty started dancing around me in excitement. Then Arthur let out a squeal in my arms and Minty froze. Then he looked up at me – *What was that?* I took Arthur into the lounge and crouched on the floor to be level with Minty. Of course, he had followed us in and was sitting and staring at us in confusion. I held Arthur towards Minty for him to have a sniff. He had a quick one, then wandered off. He didn't seem too interested.

We'd read it was important not to tell Minty to go away or dismiss him when dealing with Arthur, so even when I was feeding him, if Minty wanted to sit on my knee, I'd somehow make it work. Either Minty didn't recognize Arthur as a little human being or simply didn't care what he was.

But then I started to notice something strange. Whenever Arthur was napping in his cot upstairs, if I heard him on the monitor and went to check on him, Minty was already outside his door, waiting. He was always ahead of me, which told me that, actually, Minty understood that this tiny baby needed everybody's attention and care. He clearly felt protective of his little brother.

As Arthur grew, so did their friendship. By the time he was one, Arthur would point and clap his hands when he saw Minty. In return, Minty followed Arthur into whichever room he was playing in to sit close by. Despite all the noise and fuss associated with a new baby, Minty didn't want to be far from him.

In fact, Minty is fine with small children. After Arthur's christening, many of our friends' children were in the garden, playing and running around. Minty was in the thick of it. He loved the attention and enjoyed playing with them as much as they did with him. I knew if he'd had enough he would come inside and hide in his basket or jump onto the shed's roof, safely out of reach. We'd made sure he had lots of places to have some quiet time if he needed it. He'd mastered jumping high again and didn't seem hindered by his missing leg, although the vet had warned us that he was likely to develop arthritis in his remaining back leg later on. It was a shame but it was something we'd deal with when and if it happened.

Now Arthur and Minty are as thick as thieves. Arthur is obsessed with Minty's water bowl and likes to splash in it whenever he can get his chubby little hands on it. Minty watches patiently, assuming the role of sensible older brother. You can see him thinking,

Oh, little boy, what have you gone and done now? as water pools on the kitchen floor.

Still, we work hard to discourage Arthur from venturing too far into Minty's space – difficult when the cat flap is a source of fascination to him – but they both get such delight from rolling a ball between them. Arthur is as good for Minty as Minty is for Arthur.

Minty has enjoyed our growing family receiving more friendly visitors, and more play time, since Arthur arrived. And Arthur is growing up fascinated by and trusting in animals. We're so happy that Minty is adding this wonderful dimension to Arthur's childhood.

Having grown up thinking I was a dog person, I know now that I'm also a cat person. Getting Minty from Battersea was one of the best things we've ever done. I'm so glad I saw past my preconception that cats can be a bit standoffish, not really the home-loving animals we perceive dogs to be. Minty is an excellent example of how a cat can transform a house into a home.

We love being parents to Minty and Arthur, but it was Minty who first made us think outside ourselves a bit. Ben and I had been married ten years, enjoyed having a disposable income and the freedom to be spontaneous with last-minute holiday reservations or evenings out. When we got Minty, we thought twice about booking a holiday or even having a long day out. In a way, he prepared us for becoming a family, and now our family wouldn't be complete without him.

Cats have so much love to give. Minty's personality, and the many other characteristics we love about him, have been shaped from his having been a stray, and Battersea were able to give him a fresh start. Despite the injuries and amputation he suffered, he retained his adventurous spirit and showers us all with love every day. We never imagined a cat would change our lives so much, but he brings us immense joy and we will be grateful for ever to Battersea for bringing us together.